Inside My Pencil

Teaching Poetry in the Detroit Public Schools

Peter Markus

**DZANC
BOOKS**

DZANC
BOOKS

5220 Dexter Ann Arbor Rd.
Ann Arbor, MI 48103
www.dzancbooks.org

Library of Congress Cataloging-in-Publication Data Available Upon Request

ISBN: 978-1-941531-86-0
First US edition: March 2017
Interior design by Michelle Dotter

Portions of this book have previously appeared in *Michigan Alumnus, Teachers & Writers Magazine, Third Coast,* and *To Light a Fire: Twenty Years with the InsideOut Literary Arts Project.*

Printed in the United States of America

10   9   8   7   6   5   4   3   2   1

Contents

For Terry Blackhawk

Foreword

Because I Must: A Look Inside My Pencil

I WRITE, I AM a writer, not just because I can but because I *want* to write.

I teach writing, though, because I *must*. It's where and when I am most pure to who I am and what I was born to do. I believe this to be true.

I teach as a writer-in-residence with the InsideOut Literary Arts Project of Detroit, a not-for-profit arts organization that sends poets and fiction writers into the classrooms of inner city Detroit. I am drawn to that phrase, "inner city," because it suggests that the city is a place inside, a box inside a box, a doll inside a doll, or that there is an outer place somewhere else, but it is to the inside that I go, that I am drawn to, am taken to, by language itself.

Words have wings. That's a sentence I've heard myself and my colleagues say often here at InsideOut, the writers-in-the-schools project that has put bread on my family's table and has fed more than just my body for the past twenty-one years—a workplace where I find solace and companionship with the other writers who call InsideOut home. In the classrooms that I call home, it is not uncommon to find children who believe that they can fly, children who have "dream hands" that allow them to stand on their tippy toes and touch the moon, then take the moon in their hands as if it is a baseball and toss it spinning across the sky.

The children in these classrooms hold in their hands "magic pencils" that invite them to look inside, to look through the looking-glass that the rubbery eraser at the end of any pencil can become: a looking in, a believing in, to see the physical words—the imaginary worlds—that live at the tips of their fingers.

Here's a poem that I believe says better what I am trying to say. It's called "Jumping Words" and it's written by Chyna McKenzie, a fifth grader I had the pleasure of working with for four consecutive years.

Jumping Words

Inside my pencil
are jumping words
they are so excited
they can't wait to come out of the pencil

they're jumping on a bed

they have been drinking too much coffee
they will never stop jumping
the only way they will stop is by the pencil writing
these words are jumping every day

these words will always jump on the bed
they're happy words
they're loving words

they travel by jumping
these words will never get sad
they're jumping loving words
they hang out every day and meet new descriptive words
just like them

they will never walk
they will never run
they only jump
funny loving jumping words

that's what they are
every word loves them
every other word they meet jumps with them
they're great

their jumping makes them greater

Here, where most pencils in the world only have a thin piece of lead running through them, these kids that I teach—kids that teach me how to teach and how to see and how to be *in* the world and how to *be* my own world—they have rivers running through their pencils, they have pencils that are more than just sticks of wood, more than ordinary school supplies: their *"pencils are shooting stars burning their names across the earth,"* their pencils are *"tree trunks with roots that hold the earth where it is,"* pencils that are held by *"hands that can spell a word that will take you the rest of your life to write."* These images above (in italics) are their words, not mine. These are words—the kinds of words—that have made me into the writer I myself have come to be. These are the kinds of words that have taught me how to write, how to re-see language, how to believe and participate in a make-believe world. I am, or was trained to be, a fiction writer. But what I always struggled with, as a student, was the fiction part of any workshop. I forgot that, in fiction, as a fiction writer, we are invited to make things up and to do so in such a way that a reader might be transported, or taken hostage, or offered flight, into a world where things aren't always what they seem to be, a world of invention that doesn't have to look and be like the world that we see outside our windows. A fourth grader said it best after we read and talked about some lines from Wallace Stevens' poem "The Man with the Blue Guitar": "*For things are not what you see. / They are what you make them be.*"

I do what I do, I write what I write, teach who and what I teach, because I've learned that a classroom is more than just a classroom: a classroom is a trampoline, it is a frying pan, it is a trap door to the sublime, a rabbit hole to the eternal.

Inside My Pencil

Mr. Pete and the Twelve-Legged Purple Octopus

I WALKED INTO SCHOOL, that first day, ten minutes late.

This was no accident.

There'd been no incident or traffic jam on my way to school that morning.

I didn't wake up late.

No, I walked into school that morning, ten minutes late, on purpose.

I had a mission.

I had a story that needed to be told.

I needed to be late, though not too late, in order for this story to be told.

"Sorry, boys and girls," I said. "I'm sorry I'm so late. You're not going to believe what just happened to me."

"What?" the students wanted to know. "What happened?"

This is what happened.

No: this is the *story* of what happened.

There is, I know, a difference.

I was sitting in my car, parked on Ferry Street, the street that Golightly is located on, when I saw what I saw.

What I saw was this:

I saw, out of the corner of my eye—no, I saw it with the *whole* part of both of my big eyes—

I say this half-sentence to the kids.

Second graders.

Big-eyed.

Waiting, patiently, for me to tell them what I saw.

Waiting for me to make them see the thing that I am claiming to have seen.

That's what good writing does.

I hope to teach the students this over the next few months.

"What did you see, Mr. Pete? What was it?"

"Nah, you're not gonna believe it," I tell them. "I mean, I wouldn't believe it if it didn't happen to me."

"What? What happened? Tell us! Tell us!"

"Are you sure you want to hear it?" I ask.

"Tell us! Tell us!"

So I tell them this.

"I'm sitting in my car," I say, "right outside your school, right out there on Ferry Street, right across from your school…"

I stop.

"Does anyone in this room live on Ferry Street?" I ask.

One right hand raises.

"This happened on the street where she lives," I say, and I point at the girl with eyes that look like two moons dipped in mud.

"This happened," I say, "I saw what I saw," I say, "on the street where all of you go to school."

I am dragging the story out. I am hoping to build anticipation. Thank you for being patient.

Stay with me.

I shake my head.

I am pacing the front of the classroom.

I am part madman, part expectant father, part standup comedian.

"You're not going to believe it when I tell you." I say this sentence again. "I shouldn't even be telling you this. I should just start in with today's lesson on 'What Is a Simile?' Does anyone here know what a simile is?"

"Tell us what happened!" they chant. "Tell us what you saw!"

So much for similes, I say to myself.

I take off my sports coat to get ready: to show them that now I'm serious. It's time to roll up my sleeves and get down to business.

I roll up my shirtsleeves.

I run my fingers through my mop of hair.

"So I'm in my car," I say, "right out there on Ferry Street, not more than half an hour ago, waiting to come into your classroom to talk to you about writing poems and stories, when…"

I stop.

I shake my head.

I can't go on. I must go on.

"You're not going to believe it," I tell them.

"Tell us! Tell us!"

The students don't know it yet, or maybe they do, but they are right now engaged in the narrative act; they are caught, like fish (simile!), in the storyteller's net.

I have a captive audience.

Are you a captive audience? Or have I let you slip off the hook?

Now it's time to deliver on the promise and suspense of the story that I've been spinning.

I hope I haven't been spinning my wheels in mud.

I begin again.

The power of repetition.

Repetition is a hook.

The kids are fish (metaphor!) begging to be caught, begging to be fished into my bucket.

"I saw," I say, and I say it real slow, "a twelve-legged" (pause) "purple" (pause) "octopus" (pause) "coming toward me" (pause) "down the street."

I stop. I wait to see what these boys and girls are going to say to this.

I like to begin my teaching by embracing, by getting students to embrace, the possibilities of the impossible.

"But Mr. Pete," one boy says, and he looks up at me with eyes that are less than believing, "an octopus has only eight legs."

I tell this boy with the disbelieving eyes, this boy who has learned his facts well, this boy who has been well-versed in the anatomical details of the real-world octopus—I tell him that I know this, I tell him that I've *seen* other octopuses before (I do not use the word "octopi" because it's a word that always sounds funny on my lips when I say it), and I tell him that the other octopuses that I've seen in my life—on TV, in books, or sometimes even, as is the tradition of this hockey town, tossed out onto the ice at Red Wings hockey games—these other octopuses all had *eight* legs.

Eight legs is the norm, I tell him, and my eyes widen, as if to show him that my eyes are good eyes, that my eyes are eyes that do not lie, that my eyes are eyes that can see and count and that they know the difference between eight legs and twelve.

But this octopus, this purple octopus that I saw this morning, I say—I say it now to you—this octopus had *not* eight but *twelve* legs.

Call these legs tentacles if you like.

But I'm telling you, call them what you will, this octopus had twelve, count them, *twelve* legs: *twelve* tentacles.

I counted all twelve on both of my hands until I ran out of fingers to count on.

When I ran out of fingers to count octopus legs on, I finished counting using both of my big toes.

Ten fingers.

Two toes.

Twelve octopus legs.

I go on with my story.

So I'm sitting in my car with time to spare before I have to go in to teach, I tell them, when I see what I see.

When I saw what I saw.

I tell them that sometimes, when I'm getting ready to teach at a school, to kill time before teaching, I'll listen to some music, or close my eyes and take a short nap, or read a book, or that sometimes I'll pick up my pencil and work on writing a poem.

Or a story.

Every moment, I hope to teach them, even me just sitting in my car waiting to go in to teach, can be turned, transformed, into a poem.

My daughter, when we're walking home from school sometimes, hand in hand, or when we're at the park swinging on swings, or tossing a baseball back and forth between us, she'll sometimes say to me, because she sees the look in my eyes—it's a look that she knows well:

"Daddy, why must everything be a poem to you?"

"Because," I say to this question, "everything *is* a poem."

I hope to teach this to the students here at Golightly.

I've gotten off track a bit, I know.

But I hope that each digression is just another thread quilted into this story.

Back to that morning.

November 2, 2004.

Mr. Pete in his car.

In my car, that morning, on the car radio, that morning, there was a lot of talk about the day's elections, which, to be honest, I didn't want to hear about, so I turned off the radio and sat there in the silence of my car. I wanted to clear my head, to go into the classroom on this first day with a clean palette. I wanted to be like a freshly wiped blackboard. I wanted to be ready for their words to wash over me: to baptize me with the purity, the holiness, of their handwritten scrawl.

So I'm in my car, filled with these various forms of wanting, looking out the window, giving the neighborhood a quick once-over—there's really not much going on: no one's outside walking their dogs, no cars are pulling into the school parking lot, the school's playscape is childless—when all of a sudden, out of nowhere, I see what I see.

The twelve-legged purple octopus.

"I don't know how much you know about octopuses," I say, "or if you've even seen an octopus up close before, but this twelve-legged purple octopus, it was big."

How big?

I hope this is what the students are wondering.

"I need you to see how big this octopus was," I say.

I need *you* to see how big this octopus was.

"I wish I could bring that twelve-legged purple octopus into this room with me," I say.

"Go get him, Mr. Pete," one boy suggests.

So I take this boy up on his dare.

I go over to the classroom door. I knock on it with my knuckles.

"If I did bring the twelve-legged purple octopus into school with me," I say, "and if that octopus with twelve legs knocked with his knuckles on the classroom door, and if I were to open up this door to let him come inside..."

"Let him in, Mr. Pete!"

"Mr. Pete, open the door!"

"This twelve-legged purple octopus," I say, "it was so big," I say, "his purple head would be too big to fit in through this door."

"That's a big head," one boy says.

I nod. Yes it is.

"Now, I don't know how much you know about octopuses," I say, "but an octopus, unlike all of us," I say, "they have real soft heads."

I put my hands on top of my head and tell the students to do the same.

"Our heads are hard," I say. "But an octopus's head is soft. So soft," I say, "that if I were to get up behind that twelve-legged purple octopus, and if I were to run my right shoulder against it with all of my might, its purple head would, after a while, pop in through this classroom door."

I make a popping sound with my mouth.

Like magic, that twelve-legged octopus's big and soft purple head has popped in through the classroom door.

The students ohh and ahh.

I go on.

"And once that twelve-legged purple octopus popped his big soft purple head into this classroom, if that octopus were to walk with all twelve of its purple legs into your classroom, and if," I say, "if that twelve-legged purple octopus was tired and if it laid itself down to take a nap—even though I know that, in second grade, you're too old to be taking naps in school—but if that twelve-legged purple octopus didn't know this (because he's not in school), and if that twelve-legged purple octopus laid its big purple head down in the back corner of this classroom, using a stack of books as a pillow, and if it stretched out all twelve of its purple legs, the tips of its twelve tentacles," I tell them, "they would reach all the way to the front corner of this room, and the tips of those twelve tentacles would curl up halfway to the ceiling.

"That's how big," I tell them. I make them see it. "That's how big that twelve-legged purple octopus is."

The story, of course, does not stop there.

It is only just beginning.

I have only just begun.

Picture it: this twelve-legged purple octopus, it is anything but or-dinary, it is anything but your typical twelve-legged purple octopus.

This octopus, to begin with: it has a flair for fashion.

Look at it: on top of its big, soft, purple head rides a big, tall, smokestack of a top hat that is the color, I tell the students, of a gold-fish when sunlight lights up the goldfish's fishbowl.

Glittery.

Sparkly.

Shimmery.

Shiny.

These are just a few of the words—adjectives, adjectives! (what is an adjective, I ask: it's a word that describes a noun, I tell them)—that the students come up with to help me help them see what I saw.

Let's say that the hat riding on the top of this twelve-legged purple octopus's head is goldfish-orange.

But when I say "riding," what I mean to say is "swaying."

The goldfish-orange smokestack-shaped top hat riding atop the twelve-legged purple octopus's big soft head, it is swaying.

It is bobbling back and forth.

Why is it bobbling, why is it swaying, back and forth, back and forth?

I hope you are wondering this, too.

But first, there is something else I need you to see when I say, Picture this hat.

It is goldfish-orange.

This you already know.

And it is swaying, it is bobbling, back and forth, on top of that twelve-legged purple octopus's head.

You know this too about that hat: that it is a swaying, bobbling hat.

And sticking up from the very top of this goldfish-orange top hat on top of this twelve-legged purple octopus's head, there is a feather, big and green and fuzzy—so big that it is a feather that could not have been plucked from any bird that our eyes have ever before seen.

Do you know what a pterodactyl is?

That sort of prehistoric dinosaur-bird that used to fly, I imagine, across the prehistoric sky?

Do pterodactyls have feathers?

Did pterodactyls have feathers on their wings?

I don't know the answer to this.

But let's just say that they did: have feathers, have wings. And let's say too that pterodactyls had green fuzzy feathers covering their wings.

That's how big this green fuzzy feather is, or was.

It was so big, this green fuzzy feather sticking up from the top of that twelve-legged purple octopus's goldfish-orange top hat, that when that octopus's big, soft head swayed and bobbled, or bobbled and swayed, back and forth, back and forth, the very tip of that green fuzzy feather reached all the way down to touch the ground.

When I say "ground," I mean, of course, "cement, concrete, pavement."

This all happened on the streets of Detroit.

What is an octopus doing out on the streets of Detroit?

Don't octopuses live in the ocean, the sea?

Not this octopus.

This octopus, with its twelve legs and its big purple head with the goldfish-orange top hat riding on the top of it, it was coming toward me on the street.

On Ferry Street.

In Detroit.

The big green fuzzy feather that looked like it must have been plucked from the wing of some pterodactyl (who, or what, I have to wonder, would be daring enough, or stupid enough, to do such plucking?), it was swaying back and forth, the tip of it touching the ground, because this twelve-legged purple octopus wasn't just *coming* toward me out there on Ferry Street.

This twelve-legged purple octopus with the goldfish-orange hat with the green fuzzy feather sticking up from the top of it, it was *riding* toward me on the street.

"It was riding toward me on the street," I say, "not on a boat, not in a car, but on a unicycle."

You know what I mean when I say "unicycle"?

Or should I call it a one-wheeled bike?

That's why this twelve-legged purple octopus was bobbling its big head. That's why the green fuzzy feather sticking up from the top of its goldfish-orange top hat was swaying, back and forth, back and forth.

You have to keep your balance when riding on a one-wheeled bike, I tell them.

There is nothing to hold on to, I say, when sitting on the seat of a unicycle.

You have to use your hands, you have to hold your hands out by your sides, to keep yourself from falling.

I tell this to the kids.

I know, I say, because I've tried, three times, to ride on a one-wheeled bike.

All three times, I say, Mr. Pete fell back on his butt.

Mr. Pete is a persona.

This is something I hope to teach the kids about too.

To write from behind a mask.

To be, to become, someone, or something, else.

Flaubert once wrote, speaking about his famous book, *Madame Bovary*, and about his most famous of characters:

"Bovary is me."

I am Mr. Pete.

Mr. Pete, that's me.

I know I just said, just a minute ago, that the twelve-legged purple octopus with the goldfish-orange top hat was *riding* on a unicycle.

But "riding" is not the right word either.

This is something else I hope to get the students tuned into: to pick the best word, the rightest word, the exact word.

That twelve-legged purple octopus wasn't just *riding* down the street on that unicycle.

What that octopus was doing, out on Ferry Street—it was doing all sorts of *tricks* on that unicycled, one-wheeled bike.

I'm talking about back flips and front flips and side flips and the kinds of spins on that one-wheeled bike that you see figure skaters do out on the ice at an ice rink.

You know, like when they spin and spin around and around in a circle in the middle of the ice.

Like Dorothy Hamill used to do.

That's what that twelve-legged purple octopus was doing, not on the ice, not on figure skates, but out on the street on that one-wheeled, unicycle of a bike.

I try to get the kids to see this.

I use my words, I choose my words carefully, so that they might see what I see.

I was minding my business. I was sitting in my car. I was trying to clear my head.

This is how all stories begin.

Nothing much going on.

A man waiting to go teach and to talk about writing.

Until something else comes along to disrupt, to launch, the given situation into the land of the dramatic.

That's something else I hope to teach these students.

That in a story something has got to happen.

Even if it's something small: a boy writing his name for the first time in the snow on the sidewalk.

A father sitting up alone in the dark.

An old man on his knees in his garden.

A flower the moment it begins to bloom.

Or it could be something big that gives birth to the story: like a man waking up in his bed one fine morning to find out that he is a bug.

A cockroach.

I believe the verb in that opening sentence is "transformed."

A funny thing happened to me, a few mornings after my first encounter with that twelve-legged purple octopus with the goldfish-orange top hat with the green fuzzy feather dangling down off the top of that hat, who was riding—who was doing all sorts of tricks on—that one-wheeled bike.

I came into the classroom armed with Kafka's *The Metamorphosis* tucked (like what? a tiny football, or a secret?) underneath my arm.

I wanted to talk to the kids about the powers of the imagination, how words can get us to believe in the unbelievable.

When I walked in that morning, me and my pal Kafka, the word of the day, that day, written on the blackboard (in truth it is a magic-marker board), was the word "transformed."

A pretty big word to fit in the brains, in the mouths, of these little second graders.

But they ate it up.

We talked about how things transform, how they change, how they turn from one thing into another: butterflies, seeds, how summer turns to fall, etc.

Then I asked them what, if they could transform into anything in the world, what would that anything be.

We wrote persona poems from the points of view of butterflies and angels, dogs and cats, and, of course, octopuses, one of which, if I remember correctly, had twenty-nine legs.

But let's get back to that octopus that only had twelve legs.

That story I need to bring to an end.

Back when I was last telling you about that twelve-legged purple octopus with the big purple head and the goldfish-orange hat who was doing all sorts of tricks on its one-wheeled bike, I did not get to tell you something about octopuses that you might not know.

Octopuses, in general, and this twelve-legged octopus specifically, they don't see so good with their eyes.

This octopus was wearing glasses, big thick eyeglasses, the kind of glasses that make your eyes look even bigger than they actually might be.

Nothing, I know, I tell the students this, is ever what it seems.

This octopus's eyeglasses, they were so thick, as thick as ice needs to be out on a river or a lake for cars to be able to drive out on it—that's how thick these eyeglasses were—and because they were as thick as they were, the eyes on this twelve-legged purple octopus looked as big as moons when the moon in the sky is so big and full it looks close enough to stand up on our tippy toes to touch it with the tips of our fingers.

But even though this octopus's eyes looked big to me, they still did not see me sitting in my car.

I had my car window cracked just a little bit to let in the cool November air.

I was just getting over a cold, a cough.

I was sitting there watching that twelve-legged purple octopus spin and twist and flip and bounce up and down on that unicycle of his when, without knowing that I was doing it, I cleared the phlegm from my throat.

I made a sound with my throat, like when you make that sound with your throat to try to get someone's attention.

I do not know if there is a word to describe the sound of that sound: a grunt or groan, it isn't either one of these.

Either way, I did not want to get anyone's attention.

I did not want this twelve-legged purple octopus to see Mr. Pete.

It did not see Mr. Pete.

It—this twelve-legged purple octopus somersaulting left and right and jumping up and riding on the top edge of the fence that runs around the school's parking lot—it stopped what it was doing and it turned and looked *at* me and *through* me when it heard me make that sound with my throat.

Octopuses might not be able to see too good, but know this too: they can hear the sound of a fish swimming toward them from a mile (hyperbole, cliché!) away.

I read this somewhere in some book.

Or maybe I just made it up.

Either way, I'm putting it into this story.

That's another thing I hope to teach these kids: if you don't know, if you can't remember, make it up.

Words will find their own truths.

So in other words: I'm busted, I'm caught, sitting in my car, gawking, octopus-watching, with both of my eyes doing the looking, on this cool November day in Detroit.

I duck down behind my steering wheel so that this twelve-legged octopus might not see that it's me.

My heart is a cradle rocking in my chest, I'm so afraid.

Who knows, I tell the kids this. Maybe this morning the twelve-legged octopus skipped breakfast and maybe he'll decide to chew me up and not spit me back out.

That's what was running through my head.

A minute passes.

Maybe two minutes.

Still, I do not look up from behind the steering wheel of my car.

I am afraid of what I might see.

It's okay sometimes to be afraid, I say, even if you're a grown-up like Mr. Pete sometimes is.

After a while, after maybe five minutes of hiding like this, cowering behind the wheel, I decide to face fear in the face (cliché!).

Little by little, inch by inch, I lift myself up from behind the wheel, slowly, like a gopher or a groundhog afraid of his own shadow.

When I finally do open up my eyes, I see that I am looking, I am staring, I am gazing, straight into the face, right into the eyes, of that twelve-legged purple octopus.

This octopus does not look very happy to see Mr. Pete.

I see two moon-big eyes that are glaring.

I see the kind of a face that only a mother could kiss.

This octopus's lips are puckered up, but not puckered to be kissed.

This octopus's lips are puckered up like the way the fingers on a hand close up to make a fist.

I don't want to fight.

I am not that kind of a man.

I am not the kind of man you'd cross the street to avoid.

I'm the kind of a guy who crosses the street to stay out of trouble, even if it means almost getting hit by a car that has no headlights.

I'm not sure what to do with the look on that octopus's face.

There is a lump in my throat that makes me feel like I've just swallowed an apple, whole.

An apple a day might keep the doctor away, but it does nothing to keep an octopus from wanting to eat you.

Then I remember something that my mother once told me. My mother once said that if someone's being mean to you, if somebody, some bully at school, or a stranger you just met on the street, if that somebody is looking at you like he doesn't like you, if he or she or it is being all grumpy and is looking like they want to chew you up and spit you back out—what my mother told me to do in situations like this was *not* to look back all mean and frowny and cross-eyed at this cross-eyed person. You don't want to mirror anger, my mother liked to say. What you want to do in moments like this is smile, is send them a little dose of love.

So I listened to what my mother said.

I did my best to conjure up a smile.

I smiled a smile that was so big the smile actually made my face hurt.

Imagine that look.

I was shaking in my shoes.

But then it happened.

Call it a transformation taking place.

My mother was right (aren't mothers always right when it comes to things like this?).

The face on that twelve-legged purple octopus, the look on that octopus's purple face, turned, it changed, it was transformed, before my very own eyes, into a face that now a mother could kiss.

Yes, this octopus, when I smiled, this octopus, it smiled back.

It was a smile big enough that if this smile was a skateboard ramp, which is what this smile was shaped like, even Tony Hawk would shy away from skating down it.

Yes, it was that big.

I was happy to see that big smile on that octopus's big purple face.

But I wasn't so happy about the smell that I smelled coming from its octopus mouth.

When that twelve-legged purple octopus smiled the way that it did, one thing I learned by looking at that smile was that this octopus hadn't been to see a dentist in like two hundred and fifty years.

This octopus, it had only three teeth in its big octopus mouth: two up top near the front of its mouth, and one lone tooth barely hanging in there on the bottom. And tangled in between these teeth there were braids of seaweed and the bones of dead fish poking out from its blackened gums.

We all know that if you don't brush your teeth, even for a day, your breath can get kind of stanky-smelling. Right?

Well, after let's say even just a hundred years of not going to see the dentist, and let's say twenty years of not brushing and flossing between your teeth, as you might imagine (imagine it with me), the smell coming from this octopus's mouth smelled like _____.

I'll let you fill in that blank.

*

But this is not an unhappy story.

Even though this story does not end up smelling entirely like roses, the story does end on a happy note.

Mr. Pete and the twelve-legged purple octopus work things out.

Mr. Pete does not get eaten.

What happens is this.

Yes, I think I can give the ending away.

This story ends with a kiss.

Yes, it's true, that octopus with the breath that smelled like _____ (no, it was worse than the smell of dead fish, so go and try to find another simile), this octopus rapped with just one of its twelve tentacles on the driver's side window of my car, and so I bravely opened the door and decided to shake hands with this twelve-legged fish-eater. (Hey, I'm a fish-eater too, so I figured we had fish in common between us.)

So I stuck out my hand for this octopus to take. I was ready to shake hands with all twelve of its slimy octopus legs.

But the octopus did something else instead.

Maybe shaking hands is what only mammals like us do.

The creatures of the sea exchange greetings like this: *not* with their hands, but with their mouths.

This twelve-legged purple octopus with the goldfish-orange top hat with the green fuzzy feather sticking up from its top and the eyeglasses that made its eyes look like two moons—this octopus took me into its arms and legs, all twelve of them, and it held me like this, face to face, cheek to cheek. And then this octopus took my cheeks into just two of its twelve tentacles, the way my grandmother used to do when I'd go to visit her and she would tell me how big and handsome I was getting to be.

When my grandmother used to do this to my cheeks, I knew that a wet kiss, the kind of a kiss that only a grandma can kiss her grandkids with, was on its way.

I used to always close my eyes until this kiss was over.

So now, I closed my eyes, I plugged my nose, waiting for that octopus kiss.

You've seen or at least heard about the guy at the circus who puts his head into the lion's mouth.

Well, this kiss was something like that.

That twelve-legged purple octopus took my whole head into its mouth. And it kissed me.

I can still smell it on me to this day.

Good writing is like a kiss.

Okay, I've got a confession to make.

None of this actually happened.

I made it all up.

No, not all of it.

But most of it.

The parts about the twelve-legged purple octopus with the goldfish-orange top hat doing tricks on that one-wheeled bike, etcetera, etcetera, etcetera.

That didn't *actually* happen.

But let me be absolutely clear about one thing.

I did *see* what I say I saw.

I saw, with both of my eyes, that twelve-legged purple octopus.

I saw it doing all the things I said that it did.

I saw it on that unicycle.

I saw it doing tricks.

I saw its goldfish-orange top hat sitting on top of its big purple head.

I saw its eyeglasses.

I saw it smile.

Its teeth.

Its teeth, I forgot to mention, they were yellowish-brown, or maybe it'd be better to say that they were brownish-yellow.

I saw it kiss me.

Yes, it kissed me.

I saw all of that.

I experienced everything that I saw.

But I saw it not in the way that most people see what they see.

I saw all of this when I lifted my pencil up to my eye.

And I looked inside.

Inside my magic pencil.

Where anything—no, everything—is possible.

Inside My Magic Pencil

I HOLD UP MY pencil for everyone to see.

"Look at this pencil," I say.

I see them give this pencil of mine a look.

"It's not the most handsomest pencil in this room," I point out. "There's nothing fancy about how this pencil looks. Right?

"On the surface," I say, "this pencil looks just like any other ordinary pencil."

I walk around the room, from student eye to student eye, so that everyone in this room has a chance to see what I want them to see.

Mr. Pete's magic pencil.

"Who wants to help Mr. Pete out?" I ask.

A flurry of hands raise up before I even say what I want help with.

"Look at this pencil," I say again. "What words would you use to describe this pencil?"

I hear words like dirty, beat-up, raggedy, rusty, stubby, burnt-looking, paint-chipped.

The list goes on and on.

"It looks," one boy then says, his grin big and proud, "like it's been getting chewed on by a pitbull pup."

"Wow," I say. "Thank you. Boy oh boy, boys and girls, those are all good descriptive words to describe this pencil."

I tell them next to take a look at their own pencils, many of which have smiley faces or shimmery stars or yellow pictures of SpongeBob SquarePants on them.

"Look at all these fancy-looking pencils," I say. "There are some really beautiful pencils with us in this room."

One girl, when she sees Mr. Pete's dirty, beat-up, raggedy, rusty, stubby, burnt-looking, paint-chipped pencil with no eraser on one end and a blunt tip of lead just barely sticking out from the front of it, offers me her shiny new pencil as a gift.

"Thanks," I say, "but no thanks. I've got the only pencil I need."

My magic pencil.

I hold it up for all to see.

I give it a kiss.

"I've had this pencil for over thirty years," I tell them. "Since I was in the third grade."

"That's a long time ago," someone says.

"It must be a magical pencil," someone else says.

"It is," I say. "But it's not like how a magic wand is magical." I want them to know this. "I can't tap you twice on top of your head and make you disappear into thin air."

I tap one boy on the top of his head. He does not disappear.

"And I can't turn you into a butterfly or a bird," I tell them, and a few of them, I can see, look up at me a bit disappointed.

I keep on telling them about all the things that I cannot do with my magic pencil.

"I can't fly," I say.

"I can't use it to make money grow on trees, or to pull a white rabbit out of a black hat."

"I can't use it to dig down to China with."

"What can it do?" is the question one boy finally gets up the courage to ask.

"You want to know what my magic pencil can do?" I ask back.

Thirty heads bobble, up and down, yes, yes, yes.

I raise my pencil up to my eye.

I look inside.

I can see things with my magic pencil that nobody else in the world can see.

Anything that I want to see, if I want to see it badly enough, I can see it with my magic pencil.

"I can see my little son right now," I say.

I hold the pencil up to my eye, I tilt my head up, up toward the light.

"He's running around the house right now in his diaper," I say.

I keep watching my little boy running around the house.

I describe to them my son running, bare-footed, bare-chested, chasing after our dog.

"Uh-oh," I say softly.

"Don't do that," I say, loud enough so that everyone can hear.

"That little stinker," I say, and I shake my head like I can't believe what I'm seeing.

"What's he doing?" The students are intrigued to know. "What did he do?"

"You don't want to know," I say.

"Tell us, Mr. Pete! Tell us!"

I tell them that my little boy Solomon, who is two, just pulled off his diaper and took a pee in the middle of our house.

This gets some giggles and snickers and a few, "Ohh, that's gross!"

"I've seen enough of that," I say. "I think I want to see something else."

So I take my pencil and shake it like I'm shaking salt into a basket of French fries.

"I do this," I tell them, "I shake my pencil like this to keep the magic flowing so that I might see something new."

I raise the pencil back up to my eye.

I tell them that now, when I look inside my magic pencil, I see my granddad in his garden, rising up from his hands and knees, his thick white hair standing up, I say, like a dandelion gone to seed.

Then I tell them that my grandfather is dead, that he died a little over a month ago.

"But if he's dead, how can you see him?" someone asks.

"Good question," I say. "You want to know how?"

"How, Mr. Pete?"

"Because the people I love," I say, and I nod my head, "live forever inside my magic pencil."

The next question is not, "To be or not to be."

The question is, "To see or not to see."

"Who in this room," I say, "would like to have a magic pencil like Mr. Pete's?"

Sixty-odd eyes open wide.

Thirty-odd hands raise up the classroom roof.

"Good," I say. "Get ready."

I tell them to hold up their pencils to the light.

I tell them to hold onto them tight.

"What I'm gonna do," I say, "is I'm gonna go around the room, one by one, and I'm going to give you a little bit of Mr. Pete's magic. I'm going to tap your pencil twice," I tell them. "All it takes is two taps to get the magic going."

I tell them again to hold on tight. I tell them about the one time that I tapped this one little girl's pencil who wasn't holding on tight enough and the pencil flew out of her hand and out the window.

I tell them about another time, when a little boy wasn't holding onto his pencil tight enough and the pencil, with magic flowing through it, floated up out of this boy's hand and it got stuck, lead first, in the ceiling of the room.

I see their tiny fingers clench into knuckled fists around their pencils.

I go around the room, one by one, student by student, and I tap each pencil twice.

"Get ready," I say.

"Hold on," I tell them again.

"You ready?" I ask.

"Ready, Mr. Pete."

"Then let's let the magic begin."

The magic begins, I know—I believe—by getting the students to believe: to believe in the power and the magic of Mr. Pete's magic pencil.

"Hold up those magic pencils," I tell them.

I say, "Repeat after me."

Here I begin the chant. The incantation. The prayer. The song.

"I believe..."

I believe.

"...in the power..."

In the power.

"...of my magic pencil."

Of my magic pencil.

"When I look inside..."

When I look inside.

"...my magic pencil..."

My magic pencil.

"...I can see anything..."

I can see anything.

"...that I want to see."

That I want to see.

"When I look inside..."

When I look inside.

"...my magic pencil..."

My magic pencil.

"...I can see anything..."

I can see anything.

"...I can dream to see."

I can dream to see.

The prayer goes on.

"When I look inside..."

When I look inside.

"...my magic pencil..."

My magic pencil.

"...I can be..."

I can be.

"...anything I want to be."

Anything I want to be.

"Because I believe..."

Because I believe.

"...in the power..."

In the power.

"...and the magic..."

And the magic.

"...of my magic pencil."

Of my magic pencil.

"Inside my magic pencil..."

Inside my magic pencil.

"...anything is possible."

Anything is possible.

"And the world..."

And the world.

"...is mine..."

Is mine.

"...to make."

To make.

Picture it: thirty-odd voices crying these words out, singing these words out, repeating what I want them to believe.

It's through the power of this incantation, through the mantra of these words, through the power of this prayer, that the world of this classroom is transformed into a holy place, a sacred chapel, and the students are miniature angels in this make-believe, makeshift, magic pencil choir.

One magic pencil is powerful enough.

I tell the students this.

"But thirty magic pencils," I say, "in the same room."

I shake my head as if this is too much power for one building to take, too much magic for one man to believe.

"The world as we know it," I warn them, and I can't help but grin. "The world will never be the same."

Transformed.

Transformation.

The change, I can see it in their faces, is beginning to take place.

On the count of one, two, three, I say.

Uno, dos, tres.

It's time to take a look inside our magic pencils.

"On your mark," I say.

I tell them, "Get set."

I don't say go.

Not yet.

"Repeat after me," I say.

"I believe."

I believe.

"Believe in what?" I ask.

One boy answers, like the good listener that he is, "We believe in the power and the magic of our magic pencils."

"Give me some skin," I say, and I hold out my hand.

"But wait," I say. "I forgot to tell you something."

"What?"

I tell the students that I want them to be careful, that when they lift their magic pencils up to their eyes, I don't want them to stick or jab the pencil into their eyes. I don't want any eyeballs getting poked out and rolling around like marbles or hardboiled eggs across the classroom floor.

"This happened once before," I say. "All of these little boy and little girl eyes were all rolling around the floor and Mr. Pete had to get down onto his hands and knees and pick all of those poked-out eyeballs up and then I had to try to find which eyeballs fit into which eyeball sockets."

I tell them that it wasn't a pretty sight.

What is a pretty sight is a classroom of thirty second graders with their pencils all raised in the air, getting ready to look inside them.

Getting ready to look inside themselves.

We count to three. One, two, three. Uno, dos, tres. We lift our magic pencils up to our eyes. "If you can dream it, you can see it," I say.

I ask, "What do you wish you could see?"

We are all of us in the midst of this seeing.

Some of the students are making sounds, oohs and ahhs, as if they are seeing fireworks on the Fourth of July.

Some of the students begin talking about what they see.

"We'll all have a chance to say what we saw," I say, "but for right now, let's keep it to ourselves."

I tell them to keep looking.

"Thirty more seconds," I say.

Heads are craned heavenward.

I look and this is what I think. No, this is what I believe.

We are all in this room looking for God.

"The longer you look," I say, "the more you'll see."

I believe this is true.

"Pencils down," I say.

No eyeballs have been lost.

These boys and girls are good listeners.

Now it's time to see if they are good seers.

"Okay," I say. "That was beautiful."

I take a breath. "So," I say.

And then I ask: "Who saw something inside their magic pencil?"

Nearly all of the hands reach up.

The heart beats a little faster.

The stars, I realize, are within our fingertips' reach.

"And who," I say next, "saw something they've never seen before?"

The hands that are raised up raise up even higher.

These fish, they've taken the make-believe bait.

They've swallowed the magic pencil hook.

Not even the constellations in the sky are safe.

The poet Jack Gilbert has a line in one of his poems that seems fitting for me to fit in at this point in this story.

"We must unlearn the constellations to see the stars."

This line from Gilbert is fundamental to what I hope to do when I go into a classroom to teach.

To get the students to go, to look, to see beyond the surface of things.

To get these young seers, these visionaries, to go inside those places, those things—be it a pencil, a painting, a story, a stone—that are synonymous for that thing we call the self, the body, the heart.

This is some of what these young seers see:

I saw a man running down a dusty road until all that was left was dust.

I saw a robot with a triangle head and his eyes were like two boats and his body was like a TV and his hair was like light and his mouth was like a blue shoe and his legs were like a line and his feet were so big that one hundred people could fit under it.

I saw a river that looked like a chocolate river and the buildings looked like Snickers bars and the stars were made out of Laffy Taffy and the lights on the streets looked like ice cream cones and everybody ate everything up.

I saw a giant squid, it was purple, it had shiny teeth, it was eating a cheeseburger, it was writing a letter to Mr. Pete. It said, Dear Mr. Pete, I have a friend, his name is Bob. Your friend, Squid Joe.

I saw a tiger and a lion going to outer space. They had paper wings. The tiger didn't have a friend to play with so that's why the lion came and they became friends forever living in the same house.

I saw a huge eyeball. The eyeball was red. The white part of the eye was a rainbow.

I saw an elephant walking down the street, a dog talked to a boy with one leg, a dog in the sky with a book reading poems to the sun.

I saw a beautiful sunset and a rainbow too. We got some ice cream and then the sunset was gone. Then I saw stars and the moon with a face on it. And the moon was about to eat my ice cream cone and the man on the moon was about to eat me so I screamed and ran home in the dark.

I saw walking roses and an alien walking without breathing. I saw a flying stick up in the air, an eight-headed fish in a fish bowl walking on the sidewalk. I saw a shiny tooth jumping with a toothbrush and a man with one eye and a magic phone talking to a pony. Then I saw a girl named Lydia who looked a lot like me and whatever I did she did. And we were stuck together inside my pencil.

I saw a ninja in a black karate suit who was walking on top of a moving truck with a long stick in his hand that was brown. He was fighting bad guys. He punched someone so hard that he saw stars. Then he backflipped off the truck and landed on his feet in an alley and took off his suit and went home to be with his family.

I saw an angel up in heaven. It was a woman in a blue dress. She had white wings and white teeth. She was smiling. Her hair was yellow. She was kind to kids. She was at a school. She was the teacher. She had a wand that was long. The wand was red and gray and striped. She liked to read to the kids. And she liked to draw pictures too. She was an artist. She had black eyebrows and long legs. Her legs were skinny. She was so tall she had to duck her head because the stars might hit her. She was beautiful.

I saw Africa's night sky. It was so beautiful I heard someone singing. I know love will find a way.

I don't know what to say to this. What is there to say to this?

Mr. Pete, Mr. Poet-Man, that man I am who always has something to say, who always has a story to tell, is silenced by the bounty of these words. For me to speak now, I think this to myself (though I do not say it out loud), would almost be obscene.

To borrow again from poet Jack Gilbert: "*I dream of lost vocabularies that might express some of what we no longer can.*"

What I do say is this.

Thank you. Thank you. Thank you.

Wow. Wow. Wow.

But this is only the beginning.

"You saw," I say, "inside your pencil, a man running down a dusty road until all that was left was dust?"

The boy whose eyes took him inside that place nods his head yes.

"You mean to tell me that there's a man inside your pencil?"

He smiles and nods his head again.

"Where was he running to?" I ask.

"He was running home to see his mama," he says.

"How come he was running and not walking?" I say.

"Because his father is dead."

I shake my head.

Here again, I don't know what to say when words like these rise up, out of nowhere, and slap me in the face.

I am flabbergasted.

I am floored.

I want to lie down in some corner of this room and tuck my knees in close to my face and weep for what this boy has just now said.

No, I want to run home to see my own father and throw my arms around his neck.

I want to know more about that African night sky.

"Someone is singing," I say to the boy who saw this sky when he looked inside his magic pencil.

Who is singing?

This is the question now.

"Who is singing?" I say.

He says, "God is singing."

God is singing.

"Who is God singing to?" I ask.

"God is singing to the sky," he says.

"That's really beautiful," I say.

What else is there to say?

Sometimes silence, the sound of that sound, that momentary stillness, is the only sound that fits.

My poet-brother, John Rybicki, the most inspiring writing teacher I've ever seen teach, once wrote to me in a letter:

> *When we sing*
> *we are returning God*
> *back to God.*

Here, at this point in this story, I think Rybicki's words fit.

But it's also true that not everyone has heard the sound of God singing. And it's true too that not everyone in this room who's got a magic pencil in their hand sees something when they lift it up to their eye and look inside it.

A handful of students did not raise their hands when I asked them, "Who saw something inside their magic pencil?"

Which is okay.

Which is expected.

Sometimes you have to look twice.

I tell them all, even those who saw something the first time they looked, to take up their pencils.

"Get ready. Get set. On the count of one, two, three," I say. "Uno, dos, tres." I count us down.

"Now shake," I say, and I show them how to shake the pencil

good. "Your pencil is no longer a pencil," I tell them. "Your pencil is now a salt shaker. Shake it up," I say. "This'll get the magic flowing."

Thirty odd fists are shaking salt over baskets of imaginary French fries. There is so much salt flying around in this classroom it's as if we are trapped inside a snow globe with snow falling from the sky.

Two months from now, when it is full-on winter here in Detroit, I will ask the students to look inside a snowflake. "No two snowflakes," I will tell them, "are exactly alike." What they see, when they look inside, is further proof of this. I will also ask them questions like, What does snow falling from the sky sound like if you listen real close? What does snow falling from the sky look like if you look real close?

In short, I am inviting them to pay attention to the world around them—to see what others fail to see.

But back to those magic pencils.

So we're shaking them hard.

Salt—or snow, depending on how you want to look at it—is making a white-out blizzard of the classroom.

The magic inside those magic pencils is flowing.

It is flowering.

"Okay," I say. "Time to take a look."

But first. We need to say again the Pledge of the Magic Pencil.

"I believe…"

I believe.

"…in the power…"

In the power.

"…and the magic…"

And the magic.

"…of my magic pencil."

Of my magic pencil.

"When I look inside…"

When I look inside.

"…my magic pencil…"

My magic pencil.

"…anything …"

Anything.

"…no, everything…"

No, everything.

"…is possible."

Is possible.

You get the picture.

Words are taking us to that place.

Words, these words, chanted like this, pledged like this, are opening that door. I call it the trap door to the eternal.

The sublime.

And so we lift those magic pencils up to our eyes.

We open that door.

We take a look inside.

Hafiz, the great Sufi poet from the fourteenth century, once wrote, "*Our words become the house we live in.*"

I can't help but picture now a house made out of words.

It is a beautiful picture.

What kind of a house do we want to live in?

That is the question.

We should remember these words the next time we open up our mouths.

*

The question next is this:

"Who saw something this time when you looked inside your magic pencil?"

Here again, most of the hands raise up as if to fingertip-touch the ceiling tiles, including a couple of kids whose hands had not risen the first time I asked that question—students, in other words, whose eyes had not seen anything when they looked the first time inside their magic pencils.

I am, of course, pleased by what I see.

I do see, though, two pairs of hands that have yet to lift up from their desks.

So I see that I still have some work, some magic, left to do.

This is some of what the students saw the second time they looked inside:

I saw a nine-headed skeleton and a dragon fighting each other.

I saw a goldfish with a dark purple hat walking down the street.

I saw a monster with one eye and three legs. He was bigger than me. He could walk all the way from Michigan to China. He was bigger than fifty school buses. He was bigger than a big cruise boat. He was bigger than heaven.

I saw a monster chained up. His eyes were round and inside they were yellow and red. He had little cursive pictures on his feet. He was as big as two buildings put together. He attacked with fireballs coming out of his hands. His chains were swinging. He was knocking down houses. He knocked down the Empire State Building. He stepped on trees. He drank all the water to get more power. He destroyed every school in the world.

I saw a monster with red eyes. He was as big as this building is. He was so big if he took one step he could cross the Detroit River. He had silver wings that were made out of metal. He blew fire from his mouth. He blew fire at the Empire State Building but no one got hurt. He could jump up to heaven. He could pick up a planet in one hand. He ate the Twin Towers and then he ate the Statue of Liberty. Then he flew to Mars and set it on fire. Then he ate the Sun and he was still hungry so he ate a meteor. Then he ate every planet in the world.

I saw two men with six eyes and one foot. They had red and blue hats on and their noses were orange. Their names were Poch and Boch. They had black and red shoes on and they both had a red face. I saw a strange dog with them too. The color of the dog was red too. And I saw a monster too. He had red and blue eyes. He was scary. He was so scary that I felt like I was about to fall out of a car.

I saw a monster that blew fire at this building. He made a noise that hurt my ears. So I got a jar and put him in there but then he got out and destroyed the rest of the city.

As you can see, seeing monsters became a bit contagious. But words and pictures inspire like words and pictures.

Call it the pleasures of influence.

It's the power of language to shape the world and the way that we live in it.

The Boy with the
Blind Third Eye

BUT NOW IT'S TIME for me to work on those two sets of eyes that, both times when they lifted their pencils up, they didn't see a thing.

The one boy, when I ask him what he saw, says that he saw nothing but pencil lead on the inside of his pencil.

The other person, a girl, says all she saw was the eraser at the end of her pencil.

Okay, so I'm dealing with a couple of realists.

Degas once said that he didn't paint what he saw but what would enable the viewer to see what he wanted them to see.

I tell the girl to imagine that the eraser at the end of her pencil is a window, to imagine that her pencil isn't just a pencil: that her pencil is a telescope.

"Do you know what a telescope is?"

One boy shouts out from the back of the class that a telescope is what you look through when you want to see the moon and the stars up close.

"Exactly," I say to this.

"Let's pretend, let's make believe, that your pencil is a telescope. What kind of things would you like to see up close?"

She doesn't say anything to this. She looks up at me with eyes that seem to say, *But my pencil isn't a telescope, Mr. Freak. My pencil is just a pencil.*

"We're just making things up," I say. "We're just messing around here. There's no right or wrong answer."

Here, hearing this, her face seems to relax.

"Close your eyes," I tell her. "Everyone," I say. "Close your eyes for a minute."

I close my eyes with them.

"Who in this room," I then say, "has ever had a dream? Not a dream like you dream to one day become a doctor, but a dream like when you close your eyes at night and you go to sleep kind of a dream?"

We talk a bit here about the different kinds of dreams that we've had.

"I dreamt last night that I was flying," one boy says.

Another boy says, "I dreamt that I was walking home and I fell down into a hole."

"I had a dream once that I was trapped inside a burning house," one girl says.

To this I say, "That sounds more like a nightmare."

"It was," she says, but she doesn't seem like she's scared anymore. "But I got out."

"That's good," I say. Then I ask her, because I want to know, "How'd you get out?"

"God came and saved me," she says.

"Wow," I say to this. "That's some dream."

"Then what happened?" is what I want to know next.

"Nothing happened," she said. "The dream ended. And I woke up."

I go on. I keep on. The show must always go on.

"But the fire," I say. "The burning house. You saw it, right?"

She nods her head.

"And when you were flying in your dream," I say to the boy who dreamt last night that he was flying. "You could see yourself flying, right?"

This boy nods his head too.

"And you," I say, to the boy who was walking home and fell down a hole, "you could see the hole, right?"

This boy shakes his head no.

"I didn't see the hole," he says. "That's how come I fell in it."

Good point.

"But how about you walking home?" I say. "How about you falling down the hole? Could you see that?"

This time he nods.

"Okay," I say. "Explain this." I cross my arms at my chest. "How can you see what you say you saw, in your dreams," I say, "if you're asleep. We all sleep, do we not, with our eyes closed, yes?"

Most of the heads in the room are bobbling up and down.

"So how do we see our dreams?" is what I ask next.

There is silence: thirty seconds of silence.

I wait. Let the silence sink in.

"You want to know how we see our dreams," I say.

They do.

So I tell them.

I tell them about the third eye.

This is what I tell them.

"Look at Mr. Pete," I tell them. "How many eyes do you see?"

We go around the room.

"Where are my eyes?" I ask them to tell me.

They all point to the two eyes that are like bookends to my long and crooked nose.

I shake my head.

"Nope," I say. I suck in my lips. "You're not looking where you need to look. You're still not seeing all three of Mr. Pete's eyes."

I go slowly around the room.

"I see your third eye," I say to one little girl. "And I see your three eyes," I say to the boy sitting behind her.

"And I see yours," I say, "and yours," I say, pointing, "and I see yours and yours and yours and yours and yours…"

I see almost a hundred eyes gazing back at me here in this room.

A hundred eyes but only thirty-three bodies, including Mr. Pete.

How is that possible?

"How," I ask, "is that possible?"

You do the math.

The math doesn't work out, does it?

It does work out once you realize that we all have three eyes instead of just two.

I take my right hand and push my hair up off of my forehead.

I walk around the room for a minute like this.

"Do you see it?" I say. "Right here," I say, and I point to a point in the smack-dab middle of my forehead.

The third eye.

It's right there.

You can't see it.

But it's there.

Believe me.

I say this to the kids.

I am saying this to you.

The third eye, I tell them, is the eye that you see with when you see your dreams.

Your third eye is your dream eye.

Sometimes I like to call it that.

It is, in other words, the eye that we dream with.

It is the eye that is a bridge between us and our imaginations.

Between us and our dreams.

Our dream eye/third eye opens, I say, when we close our other eyes, like for sleeping.

"Close your eyes," I tell them again. "Lift your pencils up to this dream eye. Tell me what you see."

I see me falling down a hole but I don't get hurt because a big bird catches me before I hit the bottom.

I see me in a burning house but I get out before the fire gets me because God loves me and saves me from the fire.

I see me running on top of a rainbow and I dive into a pot of gold at the bottom of the rainbow that is filled with a million dollars.

I see me riding on the back of a dolphin and the dolphin has wings and we fly all the way up to heaven.

I see me sitting on the moon fishing for stars.

It's interesting how, in the eye of the third eye, almost all of the students see themselves as the star of their dream eye story.

Maybe it's because they are beginning to see that they are the stars, they are the heroes, of their own stories.

It's like what the French poet Edmond Jabes once wrote:

"When, as a child, I wrote my name for the very first time, I realized I was beginning a book."

I tell the kids to write these words down in their notebooks.

"These are words to live by," I tell them.

"We've all got a name," I point this fact out.

And behind every name, behind every child, there is a book, there is a story waiting to be told.

I go back to the boy who saw nothing but lead on the inside of his pencil. I ask him to tell me what he saw when he lifted his pencil up to where I've said his third eye is gazing out from the middle of his forehead.

"My third eye," he tells me, gazing up into my eyes. "My dream eye," he says, point blank, all business-like, "is blind."

This boy here with the third eye that he says is blind, he is going to be a tough shell for me to crack.

"Tell me more about your third eye," I say to this boy with the blind third eye. "How'd it get to be blind? What happened to it to cause its blindness? Were you born with a blind third eye or did it go blind all of a sudden?"

I ask these questions because I want to hear this boy with the blind third eye reach back into his own imagination and make something up.

"It got poked out," he tells me.

"So your third eye got poked out," I say. "Interesting. Very interesting." I nod my head to let him know that I believe what he has to say.

"Who poked it out?" I ask him.

"Actually," he says, "it got shot out."

Okay, this is good. This boy, he is in charge of his story. He is the one making this make-believe story up.

"Who shot it?" I ask. "Was it shot out with a slingshot, a gun, a bow and arrow?"

"A bow and arrow," he says.

"A bow and arrow," I say. "And who shot the bow and arrow? Was it some bow hunter?" I ask. "Did you go for a walk in the woods dressed up like a deer? Is that how your third eye got shot out?"

"It wasn't a hunter who did the shooting," he says. "I wasn't dressed up like a deer in the woods."

I want to keep the story moving. This boy's on a roll. He is all serious. All business. He is setting the record straight.

"So who was it, then? Who shot out your third eye?"

He pauses and gives this question some thought. I can see the gears grinding and clanking behind his two other eyes.

Then, a light goes off above his head. He has a look on his face like he is seeing something only he can see.

"Cupid," he says. "It was Cupid." He nods his head. I can see that he is pleased with the story he is making up.

"Cupid," I say. "The God of Love. Wow," I say. "That's an amazing story. And let me tell you something," I tell him. "You're not alone. I can totally relate to that story. I too have been blinded by love."

I am speaking from the heart. I am offering them a piece of my heart. It doesn't matter if they don't know it.

The offering is there.

"It's true," I go on. "Love can sometimes make the third eye go blind. But guess what?" I say. "The third eye can also grow back. It's like the arm of a starfish. If a starfish loses one of its arms, did you

know this, that arm grows back. It regenerates," I say. "Say 'regener-
ate.'" I say it real slow.

"Re-gen-er-ate."

One boy says "refrigerator."

And the whole class starts to laugh.

What I want to know now is why. Why did Cupid shoot this boy's
third eye out? What, in other words, was Cupid's motivation? To better understand a character in a story, to fully understand a story, we
need to know what makes any of us do the things we do. What makes
us tick? Makes us human?

So I ask this boy with the blind third eye, "Why?"

"Was it an accident?" I ask.

"No."

"So it was on purpose, then?"

"Yes."

"Why would Cupid do a thing like this on purpose?" I say.

"Because he was mad," he says. "Cupid was mad at me."

"But why? Why would Cupid, the God of Love, be mad at a
little boy like you?"

I really do want to know what he thinks.

"Because," he says, and here he hesitates, "I said something that
I shouldn't have said."

"What? What did you say?" I say. "What could a little boy like
you possibly say that would make Cupid, the God of Love, so mad
at you that he'd shoot out your third eye, your dream eye, with his
bow and arrow?"

He looks up at me with a glint of sadness in his big black eyes.

I wait.

The whole class is waiting.

Are you waiting too?

Good.

What this boy said was this.

"I said," he says, "that I didn't love my mama."

"I said," he says, he confesses this to the whole class, "that I hated my mama. That's why Cupid did what he did."

When he says this, the tears on his beautiful face make his face look even more beautiful.

I put my hand on his shoulder. Then I hold out my hand for him to shake.

"Give me some skin," I say. I tell him, "It takes a big person to admit when he's said something that he knows now that he shouldn't have said. And guess what? Cupid forgives you. Your mama forgives you."

"No she doesn't" is what he says to this.

"Of course she does," I tell him. "Your mama loves you. Even if you said that you didn't love her, she would still always love her little boy."

As a father, as a son, I believe this to be true.

"No she doesn't" is what he says to this.

And then what he says next is something I am not prepared to hear. I don't know what to say to this.

What he says is, "My mama doesn't love me," he says, "because," he says, staring up at my face, "my mama is dead."

He says, "She died."

He shakes his head. "That's why the eye in the middle of my head can't see nothing."

*

But of course, sometimes nothing *is* something. Sometimes we say nothing is wrong when there's really a whole lot of something going on. Sometimes we say we have nothing (because sometimes we feel like this is true) and yet us having nothing becomes a fullness that only a poem is sometimes able to articulate. Such as in this poem by one of my high school students, appropriately titled "Nothing":

Nothing

Nothing
I have nothing

Nothing
Only nothing

Nothing
Except you.

The boy with the third eye shot out and blinded by Cupid's revenge-tipped arrow gave me more than he knew that morning. Not only did he give me a piece of his heart torn out by its roots, an image that always makes me think of the Stephen Crane poem about that mythical desert creature who eats his own heart, he also reached down into a space beyond the heart, into his soul, down into his core child self, to bring back out into my world the story of a vengeful Cupid who is, in this boy's refashioning of the myth, more of a god of retribution and punishment than he is a god of love.

Here's the poem by Stephen Crane that I mentioned above. It is a poem that bears no title, a poem that for me speaks directly to the art and heart of poetry, a portrait of the poet who has gone off into the wilderness and is now returning with his subject in his hand, driven to this place by the art of hunger.

> *In the desert*
> *I saw a creature, naked, bestial,*
> *Who, squatting upon the ground,*
> *Held his heart in his hands,*
> *And ate of it.*
> *I said, "Is it good, friend?"*
> *"It is bitter—bitter," he answered;*
> *"But I like it*
> *Because it is bitter,*
> *And because it is my heart."*

"*If I could do it, I'd do no writing at all here.... A piece of the body torn out by the roots might be more to the point.*"

That's James Agee speaking, in *Let Us Now Praise Famous Men*, about his subject: the men and women and children of sharecropper Alabama circa 1936.

My subject here in this book, some eighty years later, is the schoolchildren of Detroit, but Agee's words seem to fit like a glove, or a glass slipper, or a muddy boot. Yes, like a muddy boot.

A piece of the body torn out by the roots.

A piece of the heart.

But a piece is not enough.

I tell this to the students.

You have to put your whole heart, you have to throw your whole body into the writing of a poem or story. This is a portrait of writing as a sport, a physical activity, not unlike football or basketball or running track.

I call myself the P.E. instructor here at Golightly.

No, not the classic Physical Education guy. Not the gym coach.

P.E. as in Poetic Educator.

Which, like I've said, poetry is its own sport.

Everything that you've got to give, during the writing of the poem or story or book, must be put into that poem or story or book.

I'm talking both emotionally and physically.

I'm talking spiritually.

Give speech to the spirit, to the heart.

Give speech to those words that are stuck in your throat waiting for you to say them.

"*Insist, insist, until I at least fail,*" the poet Jack Gilbert writes.

Or in the words of Beckett: "*Ever tried. Ever failed. No matter. Try again. Fail again. Fail better.*"

It's true, on the page, anything—no, everything!—is possible.

I believe this.

Though I know, too, that nothing is ever enough.

This is the poet's paradox.

Nothing is ever enough.

The poem must not just capture life, or mirror life.

The poem must take on a life of its own.

The poem must be a life.

The poem must be bigger than life.

The poem must make more sense than real life.

Real life, I tell them, rarely makes sense.

The poem on the page makes sense of that senselessness that we call life.

Life.

Death.

Everything in between.

Never use the word "life" in a poem.

It's too vague, I tell them.

It means too many things to too many people.

But the poet, too, I tell them this, must be willing to break the rules.

Go ahead and use the word "life" in a poem.

Be lawless.

Be outrageous.

Be anything you want to be.

The thing perhaps is to eat flowers and not to be afraid.

This is e.e. cummings talking.

Be afraid of nothing, I tell the students.

Tell it like it is.

Be outrageous and lawless.

Be a liar.

Be a thief.

T.S. Eliot: "*Good poets imitate. Great poets steal.*"

But remember too, I tell them. Don't be afraid to be tender. Don't be afraid to put flowers in your mother's hair.

Back to the boy whose third eye was blinded by Cupid's retributive arrow.

After I left school that day and was in my car heading home, I couldn't help but wonder, How well did this little boy know his mother? How well did this little boy's mother know her little boy?

Which then led me to wonder, How well do I know my own mother? How well does my own mother know me, her own son?

This led me to remember a line from Norman Maclean's novella *A River Runs Through It.*

"*It is those we live with and love and should know who elude us.*"

The narrator, looking back over the tale he has just told, then adds, "*Now nearly all those I loved and did not understand when I was young are dead, but I still reach out to them.*"

How does he "still reach out to them"?

With words.

Stories.

More precisely: through the story we've just read when we reach these lines at the end of this book.

The boy with the blind third eye, I tell myself, can reach out to his dead mother with his words, his poems.

His song.

Which will be her song in his singing.

On the radio that day, on my way home from teaching these Go-lightly second graders about the magic inside their pencils, a song by the Flaming Lips comes on the radio, the singer crooning out of tune, "*Do you realize that everyone you know someday will die? And instead of saying all of your goodbyes. Let them know you realize that life goes fast. It's hard to make the good things last. You realize the sun doesn't go down. It's just an illusion caused by the world spinning around.*"

The sun, I see, even though it's only three thirty, already seems to be going down. And I am spinning, my head is spinning, after this day of spinning, all day long, the tale of the twelve-legged purple octopus with the goldfish-orange top hat with the green fuzzy feather swaying, back and forth, back and forth, from this purple octopus's big purple head as he rode, no, as he did all sorts of tricks—back flips and side flips and front flips and triple spins—on his one-wheeled unicycle of a bike.

When I get home, I can hardly talk—my throat is so parched.

When my wife asks me, "How'd your first day go?" I want to tell her that miracles took place in the classroom today. I want her to see, to experience, what it looks like to see thirty-odd pencils raised in the air, to see thirty-odd sets of eyes looking, squinting, to see inside their magic pencils. I want to share with her the magic of this day. I want to tell her about the boy whose third eye was shot out blind by Cupid. I want to read her some of the sentences that these tiny second-grade hands squeezed out from their pencils. I want to tell her that this is why I do what I do.

What I tell her is this.

I say, "It was okay. It was a good day," I tell her. "The kids were very sweet."

Then I say, "Kiss me."

We kiss.

But then my wife wipes the kiss away.

"Your breath," she says, and she makes a face. "Do you talk to your mother with that breath?"

Halitosis is a joke between us.

"Who have you been kissing?" she asks.

I grin and shake my head. "You don't want to know," I tell her.

*

That night, I pick up the phone and call my mother. I want to tell my mother that I'm glad she is alive, that I feel lucky she didn't die when I was still just a little boy. (She almost did die when I was nine, when a can of paint fell on her face as she stood holding onto a stepladder, but that's another story.)

What I do say is, "How was your day?"

My mom tells me about going shopping, how she had to get a prescription filled for my father, and how she thinks my father is coming down with the flu.

I hear this story, or a version of it, often.

I listen, this time, as if it is the first time.

I ask my mother questions that I already know the answers to: what store, what kind of a prescription, what are my father's symptoms.

She asks me did I vote. I ask did she and my father vote, even though I already know that they both filled out absentee ballots weeks ago.

"I've got a bad feeling," my mother tells me.

For the moment, I'm just happy to hear my mother's voice there on the other end of the line.

"Did you work today?" she asks me.

By work I know she means teach.

"I did."

"How was it?"

"Good," I tell her. "It was a good day."

I should tell her more, but I don't.

My mother says, "Did you eat?"

Like many mothers, my mother seems to think that her grown son is incapable of feeding himself. I used to find this belittling and tedious, but now I simply find it heartening to hear her ask me this.

"Yes, Mom, I ate."

I want to make an inside joke out of this question and tell her that I went out to lunch at Greektown, that I ate fried calamari (i.e. octopus). But I don't. I let it go at that.

"I better get going," I say, after a while of this.

"Have a good night," my mother says.

"I'll talk to you tomorrow," I tell her.

And to this my mother says what she always says when I say a thing like this. What she says is, and here her voice is already beginning to trail away from me, she says, *"Isten legyen veled."*

God be with you.

That night I dream about a woman who walks up to me out of nowhere and kisses me on the cheek.

She doesn't say anything, but she gives me a look, the kind of a look that says more than words ever could.

It is a look of thanksgiving.

I wake up out of this dream believing that I know who she is, that we've met someplace before.

But I can't say where exactly.

I carry this mystery with me all the next day.

I am trying to tell my wife about the boy with the blind third eye when it hits me.

That's who she is.

That's the woman from my dream.

The boy with the third eye shot out blind by Cupid: it was his mom who kissed me on the cheek.

It was his mom who looked at me with those thanksgiving eyes.

It was his mom who was saying to me, not with words, but with the look that she looked at me with, Thank you.

Thank you is what I find myself saying to the students when they say what they say, when they write what they write.

Thank you.

It's what you say, my mother taught me, when someone gives you a gift.

These kids, their words, that's what they are, every last one of them: gifts.

So let me say it again, and I know it won't be the last time that I say it, these words: Thank you.

Transformed, or On Becoming
a Ladybug

When I go back to Golightly the next week, I thank the students for being such good listeners to the story that I told them about my run-in last week with that unicycle-riding, twelve-legged purple octopus.

"Did you see the twelve-legged purple octopus today?" they ask.

"No, not today," I say.

"Tell us another story, Mr. Pete," they say.

"Okay," I say, "but first, I need to give you a test."

"No, not a test," they moan and groan. "We hate tests!"

"Tell us a story, tell us a story!"

"Do you want to know what I saw today in my magic pencil?" one boy asks me.

"I'd love to," I say, "but first…"

"I saw," this boy goes on, cutting me off quick, "I saw Mr. Pete and I saw the twelve-legged purple octopus."

So I go ahead and put the test on the back burner, for now.

I go with this boy inside his magic pencil.

"What were we doing?" I ask him.

"Mr. Pete was sitting in his car," he says, "and the twelve-legged purple octopus was doing tricks on his unicycle."

"How big was that octopus?" I ask him.

"It was big," this boy says.

"How big?" I say. "If he walked into this classroom, tell me how big this octopus would be."

"He was so big that if he came into this classroom and if he laid down to take a nap and if he stretched his legs, he'd stretch all the way from one corner of the room all the way to the other corner."

"I see," I say. "That's pretty big. Now," I say, "tell me about his head. What can you tell me about that purple octopus's head."

"He was wearing a hat," this boy tells me.

I say, "Tell me something about that hat."

"It was orange," he says, and I can tell that he's seeing it, "and it had a feather sticking up from the top of it."

"What kind of a feather?"

"It was green."

"Anything else?"

"And furry."

Another boy raises his hand and says, "Mr. Pete, the word you used to describe the green feather was fuzzy."

"Fuzzy, furry." I push out my bottom lip. "That's pretty close."

Then, "What else can you tell me?" I say. "Who," I say to the whole class, "can tell me about the color of that hat?"

"It was orange," says the boy who is telling me about what he saw inside his magic pencil.

"How orange?" is what I say to this. "Orange like the sun?" I say. "Or orange like an orange that you eat?"

A handful of hands rise up in the air.

"Orange like a goldfish!" they say.

"Good," I say. "What else can you tell me about that goldfish-orange hat?"

"It was shiny."

"It was shimmery."

"It was glimmery."

"Hey," I say, "those words rhyme."

"It was sparkly," says another.

"What else? Keep going," I tell them. "Stay," I say, "with that twelve-legged purple octopus's hat. What kind of a hat was it?"

One boy says it was a cowboy hat.

"Kind of," I say, "but I don't think Mr. Pete called it that, did he?"

It's always kind of strange hearing myself talk about myself in the third person. But I do like the effect that it has, as if the writer me, the storyteller me, Mr. Pete, is somehow different than the man I am when I go home and take off my writer hat and turn back, as if by magic, into dad, husband, son.

"It was kind of like," one girl says, "a Cat in the Hat kind of a hat."

"Yes it was," I tell her. "And do you remember what Mr. Pete called that hat? Did I give it a name?"

I think I did, but I'm not so sure.

"You called it a top hat," one boy reminds us, and he is right.

"I did call it that, didn't I?"

"You said it was kind of shaped like that smokestack," this boy says, and he turns and he points out the classroom window to the smoke-billowing incinerator rising up right across the freeway.

"Thank you for remembering that," I say.

The story, the twelve-legged purple octopus, he is coming back to me, he is coming back to us. I can almost see him in the room with us: his big purple head, his goldfish-orange top hat with the green fuzzy feather swaying, back and forth, back and forth, from the top of his smokestack-shaped top hat.

"What else do you remember?" I ask them.

They tell me, in no sequential order, about his stanky breath, about the seaweed and the bones of fish stuck in between his three teeth. They tell me about me, Mr. Pete, sitting in his car (my car), crouched down behind the steering wheel, afraid that this purple octopus was going to eat me, Mr. Pete, the both of us, though of course we are one. They tell me about what happened at the end of all of this—the wet kiss that was like sticking my head into the mouth of a lion, though maybe I should have said into the mouth of a sea lion, or maybe the mouth of a whale, an allusion to one of my all-time favorite stories, the story of *Pinocchio*, the boy puppet who turns, magically, miraculously, into a real boy, a transformation that is triggered by the love between father and son.

I am amazed by how much they remember. I am amazed by how the words have stuck. A lot can happen in the course of a week. A lot of information passes by our ears. New words, new stories. Call it, at its worst—news on the radio, the TV—static. White noise. The hum and buzz of being alive.

"Give yourselves a pat on the back," I tell them. "You guys really listened well."

"Tell us a new story, Mr. Pete."

"Okay," I tell them, and I take in a deep breath. "But you're not gonna believe me when I tell you."

I dig into my trouser pocket.

I pull out my hand with my pencil hiding inside.

"Last night," I begin. "It was late."

I stop the story there.

Shake my head.

I say, "You're not going to believe what happened."

I like to stay up late. I like to write in the dark. I'm writing these words right now in the dark. I like it when the blank white page is the only source of light. I like to wait to see which words are going to take me by the hand, to lead me, as if I am a blind man, to the other side of the street, the other side of a city where nobody knows my name.

Last night, I tell them, late, it was almost midnight, I was working on a new storybook idea about a ladybug who flies around the world, from person to person, and whoever this ladybug lands on, as ladybugs often like to do, this ladybug brings these people good luck. That, I tell them, is the basic premise, the basic starting point, the basic plot (even though plot, for me, is kind of a dirty word) of this story.

"I really like that idea, Mr. Pete," one girl tells me, which, of course, hearing her say this makes me happy and it gives me hope that the story might grow from just an idea into a bona fide book.

"Thank you," I tell her. "But listen. This is the strange part. This is the part of the story that you're not going to believe. Even if I wrote it down, into the story, which I don't think I'm going to do, even then you wouldn't believe it."

Once again the chorus, "Tell us! Tell us, Mr. Pete!" lifts my heart and so I give in and get ready to tell them last night's story.

This is what I tell them.

So I'm up late working on this story about this ladybug who brings people good luck and I've gotten maybe about halfway through the story when the darkness of night starts to get the best of me and my eyes start to get heavy-lidded and it starts to get kind of hard to see the paper and it's hard too for my hand to even hold onto my pencil and the words start to slow down a bit and so I tell myself, I say, "Mr. Pete," I say, "you've got a pretty good start to the story, so why not get a good night's sleep, we've got to teach in the morning and we don't want to be too tired for that."

So I go to bed.

Before I go to bed I go and I give my kids a kiss goodnight.

I say a prayer.

I kiss my wife goodnight.

I close my eyes.

I sleep.

Nothing strange, nothing too hard to believe, right?

"This is where things get a bit weird," I tell them.

I wake up, the next morning, alone in bed, which is not unusual since my wife usually gets up at 3 a.m. to meditate and paint. What is unusual is this: I'm in bed, on my back, and I can't get up.

"I can't get up," I tell them, "because…"

Here again I stop. I'm shaking my head. They're going to think I'm crazy. One of these kids is going to go home and tell their mom or dad about what I'm about to tell them happened to me and they're going to come to school next week, the guys in the white coats, and they're going to take me away. They're going to lock Mr. Pete up in a room with padded walls. They'll throw away the key.

"It's crazy," I say. "You're going to think I'm nuts."

"Tell us! Tell us, Mr. Pete! You're not nuts!"

Little do they know, I think.

"Thank you," I say. I go on with my story.

So I'm on my back, in bed, unable to get up out of bed, because, (I pause) because, I wake up (pause) to find myself, (pause) Mr. Pete, the man that I am (hesitate), the man that you see standing here right now, I have been transformed, I have, overnight, sometime during the night, as if by magic, I have turned, I have become…

I stop right there.

"What! What! What!"

"Can anyone guess?"

"Tell us! Just tell us."

"Are you sure you won't think I'm crazy and throw rocks at me and think I'm a freak?"

"We promise, Mr. Pete."

"Okay," I say. "I guess I'll just have to trust you on this."

And then I tell them this: that when I woke up and when I found that I was unable to get up out of bed, it was all because…

I rub my fingers through my beard.

"Tell us!"

"I was transformed…"

"…into…"

"…a gigantic…"

"…ladybug."

"Cool."

"Awesome."

"No way."

"I want to wake up to be a ladybug."

"No, you don't," I say to this.

And I tell the little girl who says this why she does not want to wake up one fine morning to find herself transformed into a gigantic ladybug.

Hats off here, of course, to Kafka.

I was stuck on my back with my skinny ladybug legs sticking out from the sides of my ladybug shell, and now I knew how those roly-poly pillbugs used to feel when, as a boy, I used to turn over rocks, down by the river, and pick them up until they'd roll up into a little ball and then, when I'd put them back down, into the dirt, they'd usually end up on their back with their little legs working like mad, trying to run, though there was nothing, nothing beneath them, to run on.

"What did you do?" one girl asks, and this, of course, is the question that needs an answer, because obviously I am here, standing in front of them, and no, I am not a ladybug, I am just Mr. Pete, a regular-looking (that's a polite way to say it) sort of a man who is here at Golightly to teach these kids about, to get them writing their own, poetry. Or, as my daughter used to say, her daddy "teaches poems," which I like the sound of that, as if I actually teach poems, or teach a poem how to be a poem. There's something simple, and yet mysterious, and of course magical, about that.

"I'll tell you what I didn't do," I tell her, "at least not at first." And what I tell her is that I did not call out for help.

"Why not, Mr. Pete?"

And so I tell them that, for one, I didn't want to wake up my kids, both of whom were still sleeping. And number two, I didn't know what my wife would do if she came into the room to find a ladybug lying in our bed.

"I tried turning over myself," I tell them. "I tried to reach out to grab hold of the edge of the bed," I say. "But guess what—in case you never noticed, a ladybug's legs are pretty short, and so I reached but I couldn't reach nothing to grab hold of.

"So I kicked," I say. "I shook my head back and forth, back and forth, until it banged up against the headboard of my bed."

I kicked and I flailed and I did my best to roll out of bed, but nothing I did did anything to get me unstuck from my bed.

"So I called out for help. I said, in my softest voice, so as not to wake up my kids, since I didn't want my kids to see me like this, I said, 'I can't get up. I need help.'"

But nobody heard me.

So I lay there for a minute or two and then I didn't just call out for someone to help. This time I yelled, "Help me!"

My wife was the first to come into the room to find me, Mr. Pete, her husband, the father of her two kids, transformed into a gigantic ladybug.

When I say that my wife screamed, I mean that my wife screamed. I mean it was the kind of a scream that is heard and described near the end of the Denis Johnson story "Car Crash While Hitchhiking," where the wife of a man killed in a highway car wreck finds out that her husband is dead.

> "*The doctor took her into a room with a desk at the end of the hall, and from under the closed door a slab of brilliance radiated as if, by some stupendous process, diamonds were being incinerated in there. What a pair of lungs! She shrieked as I imagined an eagle would shriek. It felt wonderful to be alive to hear it!*"

It didn't, for me, feel "wonderful to be alive to hear it." If anything, it seemed to make the shell on my back crack. At least that's what it felt like to me.

True, I was alive, but I was a ladybug.

Was I a man ladybug or a woman ladybug?

I didn't know. I didn't know how to tell the difference.

I said so to the boy who asked me this question.

So what did I do?

I knew I needed to calm down my wife, who, you should know, doesn't like bugs to begin with. She especially doesn't like it when bugs get in the bed with her. Or, as was the case here, bugs that wake up in her bed.

"It's okay, honey," I told her. "It's just me. Just listen to me."

And then I told her what I believed had happened during the night.

What I believed had happened was this:

I often tell my students, when they are writing a story or a poem, that they must become whatever it is they are writing about.

If you're writing a story about an old man walking with a limp down a dusty Mississippi back road, you must become that old man walking with a limp down that dusty Mississippi back road.

If you're writing a poem about a stone, or a tree, or a river, you must become that stone, or tree, or river.

If you're writing a storybook about a ladybug who flies around the world bringing good luck to whoever it lands on, then you must become that ladybug.

That's what happened.

That's the power of the magic pencil.

It's true you can become, you can imagine being, whatever you want, but you also have to be careful what you wish for: be careful of what you write about. Be careful of what you must become.

I tell this to the students.

I should have told this to myself.

This wasn't the first time something like this happened to me.
Once, a few years ago, I wrote a story called "On Becoming a Bird."
When I wrote this story, a story about a boy who, when he grows
up, wants to become a bird, I woke up one morning to find myself
transformed into a bird. Not some sissy songbird of a bird.

But a pigeon.

That's the kind of bird I turned into.

Here's the story that, because I imagined what it might be like to
be a boy who becomes a bird, and because the boy in the story wants
to become a bird when he grows up, I became a bird too.

On Becoming a Bird

*One day he decides that he wants to be a bird. Not a fire-
fighter or an astronaut or a doctor or even a nurse. But a
bird! That's nice, honey, his mother tells him. Now go watch
TV. But his father wants to know what kind of bird. The
boy gnaws on his bottom lip. What kind of a bird? Yeah,
you know, his father replies. A robin? A sparrow? A black-
bird? A crow? The boy cocks his head off to the side. He looks
up at the ceiling as if it's the sky. After a while he turns to
his father and says, I've made up my mind. A pigeon. That's
the kind of bird I want to be. His father considers the boy's
decision. Whispers the word, pigeon. He pauses. Shrugs. He
hawks his brow. A pigeon, he figures, is a classic, blue-collar
bird. Nothing fancy. Not some sissy songbird. Okay, he tells
his son. But wait here. He puts his hand on the boy's shoulder. Says: I got something to give you. The boy looks on in
silence as his father disappears into the kitchen. He hears*

the metallic click of his father's lunch-bucket lid flipping open. When his father returns half a minute later, his right hand is clenched into a fist. Here, his father says. And opens his hand. The boy opens his eyes to find a palmful of bread crumbs. He doesn't hesitate, he doesn't wait for any of the others to join in. He lowers his head, as if in prayer, and begins to eat.

When I turned into a bird, it wasn't so bad. I'd always wanted to know what it would be like to fly. So I flew. It was a beautiful day. The sky was blue. The grass, from a bird's eye view of things, never looked so green. But after a while of being a bird, I missed being just a man. So I flew back home and I turned back into Mr. Pete.

How did I do this? How did I turn back?

It was pretty simple.

My magic pencil.

That's what turned me into being a bird. And that's what would turn me back into being a man.

So I told my wife to go into my trouser pocket to get my magic pencil. I told her to put the pencil into my hand (which was more of a claw, or a pincher). The hardest part for me was holding the pencil. But I held it and I lifted it up to my right eye. I looked inside it. I wished that I was *not* a ladybug, *not* a bird, but just a man. A man who sometimes goes by the name of Mr. Pete.

Like magic, I turned back.

Back into just a man.

Good old, plain old Mr. Pete.

"Did that really happen?"

"See," I say to this. "I told you you wouldn't believe me if I told you what happened." I look kind of sad-eyed when I say this.

"I believe you, Mr. Pete," one girl says.

Someone else says, "I believe you too."

"You want proof?" I ask the rest of them, doubters, un-suspenders of disbelief.

I turn back around. I reach up with my right hand and I yank down the shoulder of my T-shirt.

Back here I have a birthmark, call it a mole, the size of a silver dollar.

"See," I tell them. "I've even got the black spot on my back to prove it."

Even the doubters in the bunch (and there are a few), I watch as their already big eyes get bigger with belief.

"So," I say. I look around the room. "Who's ready to be transformed?"

These kids are fearless and up for anything at this point.

"If you could be anything in the world," I say, "what would that anything be?"

I introduce to them the power of the verb "to be."

That is, I am.

I am is better than I wish.

I am is better than I want.

I am.

I am a ladybug.

I am a ladybug flying around the world.

I am a ladybug flying around the world bringing good luck to everyone I land on.

I am a bird.

I am a bird eating bread crumbs out of a father's hand.

I am a tree whose leaves have all fallen.

I am a stone that a boy picks up and skips across the river.

I am a river where fish with wings fly across the sky at the bottom of this river.

"Picture what you want to be," I tell them.

"See yourself transformed as whatever it is you wish to become."

"It could be anything."

"You can be anything."

I say this to the kids.

This is what they say, this is what they see:

I am the moon glowing at night.

I am a poem singing.

I am a star reading a book.

I am a book in a little kid's hand.

I am a snowflake melting on a little girl's tongue.

I am a cloud shaped like a dragon.

I am a bear looking for honey in the woods.

I am a blue moon sitting on the top of the world.

I am a black hole in the sky.

I am a god in the sky. I am a good god.

I am a happy monkey swinging on a tree.

I am a pumpkin shooting out seeds at the man with the knife who is getting ready to carve me up.

I am a tornado twisting to Orlando turning all the buildings into wires and fires.

I am the sun. I shine all day long. I keep the Earth warm.

I am a flower in bloom.

I am a butterfly flying in the neighborhood of make-believe. I can feel the breeze against my wings. I can smell the jasmine flowers.

I am a red fish swimming in a river.

I am a rock down by the river.

I am a blue river flowing through Detroit.

I am a shiny ball rolling down the street.

I am a black panther running around in Africa.

I am a horse with long flowing hair.

I am a black and deadly spider who is as big as the Empire State Building.

I am a wild lion chasing away hunters with my sharp teeth and bright eyes that are as wide as a skyscraper.

I am a yellow star shooting across the sky.

I am a yellow moon talking to the stars.

I am a blue bird flying in the blue sky.

I am a clear drop of rain falling from the sky. I am the rain singing.

I am a shell with a pearl inside it.

I am a flag whose stars are moons and whose stripes are roads leading me home.

I am an angel with white wings that sparkle. I live in the sky with a crow that is blue.

I am a blue whale swimming in the ocean. I am waving to people in a boat. I have a mouth that is shaped like a jump rope.

I am a tiger whose whiskers are trees.

I am a bird whose wings are butterflies and whose feathers are dollar bills.

I am a yellow dog barking at the birds.

I am a bird in the sky flying over houses and mountains, waking up the neighbors with my song.

I am this bird that flies high inside the sky until you cannot see it.
I am an angel who is my mother smiling from above.

This last one, "I am an angel who is my mother smiling from above," is from the pencil, from the mouth, of the boy with the third eye shot out blind by Cupid's arrow.

He is the last to speak, the one student who does not want to share, who, when I ask him what would he like to be if he could be anything at all, all he says, at first, is, "I don't want to be anything."

"You're already something," I say. "You're a boy, right?"

"Yeah."

"And not that we don't like being the boy or girl that we are," I tell him, "but sometimes it can be a lot of fun to think about what it'd be like to be something besides ourselves, don't you think?"

He shrugs.

"If I could turn you into your favorite animal, with a wave from Mr. Pete's magic pencil, what would that animal be?"

"A dead rat," he says, his voice flat and matter-of-fact.

I try a different approach. A more traditional way into his world of dreams.

"What," I ask him, "do you want to be when you grow up?"

"I don't know."

"Have you ever given that much thought?"

"Not really."

"When I was your age," I tell him, "all I ever wanted to be was a professional baseball player. I used to pray to God every night, 'Please, God, let me be a professional baseball player when I grow up.'"

"What happened?"

I tell them about how, in my senior year in high school, I hurt my arm throwing too many curveballs. I could hardly even raise my hand in class, let alone hold and throw a baseball ninety miles an hour. So I picked up the next best thing: a pencil.

"I became a writer," I tell them, "so that I could become more than what I am."

The boy with the blind third eye, he looks at me with eyes that look like they've seen too much—too many curveballs thrown his direction—in these too few years. But I can also see that, in his silence, he is becoming, he is beginning to be, something other than the boy that he is.

I am tempted to step back, to give him some space, to leave him alone until next week, let him become, in his own head, whatever it is he is becoming.

When I announce to the class that "Mr. Pete has got to go," the boy with the blind third eye raises his hand.

"I want to be an angel when I grow up," he says.

"An angel," I say. "That's a nice thing to want to be."

I tell him, "Say, 'I am an angel.'"

He does like I say.

"I am an angel."

"Now tell me," I say, "tell me something else I need to know about this angel that you want to be. Begin, again, 'I am an angel.'"

"I am an angel who is my mother."

When I don't know what to say, I often become a parrot who resorts to repeating what's just been said.

"'I am an angel who is my mother.'"

I grin big and bob my head, up and down, up and down.

I am a bobble-headed doll.

"What's this angel who is your mother doing right now?"

I want to know the answer to this. I want to see what this boy is seeing through his blind third eye.

"She's smiling," he says. "She's smiling."

He says it twice. The second time sounds even sweeter than the first.

"I am an angel," I say, "who is my mother," I say, "smiling."

I get down on my knees in front of this boy. I am seeing him, for the first time, eye to eye.

"Where are you? Where is this angel?"

"Up there," he says, and he looks up.

"In the lights?"

"Above the lights," he says to this. "Above the sky. Up in Heaven," he says.

"Let me see if I've got this right," I tell him. "You want to be an angel who is your mother, who is smiling from above the lights and above the sky, up in Heaven?"

"I am an angel," he says, "who is my mother," he adds, "smiling from above."

I get up off my knees. I hold out my hand for him, this angel, to shake it. "It's a pleasure to meet you," I say.

His hand in my hand is a baby bird in a nest.

I hold his hand but not too tight.

Bones, I know, are not the only things that can break.

I can't help but think of that James Wright poem about the horses on the side of the road just off the highway in Rochester, Minnesota.

The poem is called "A Blessing."

I know that this is not Minnesota.

This is Detroit.

There are no horses here just off the highway for us to watch grazing on grass.

There is only this roomful of tender-eyed second graders who are munching on the words of the day.

I am.

To be.

Transformed.

But nonetheless, I feel the way that the speaker in that poem feels when, at the end of the poem, he tells us that:

> *Suddenly I realize*
> *That if I stepped out of my body I would break*
> *Into blossom.*

In other words, I would become other than, he would become more than, just a man, just a man, just a man.

> *I am large.*
> *I contain multitudes.*

So said Walt Whitman.

I want to teach these kids more than just how to write a poem. I want them to learn, I want them to remember and to take away from their experience with me, more than just what a simile is, or a metaphor, or an image, etcetera, etcetera.

All that's just the technical side of the poem: the nuts and bolts and screws.

They can learn that anywhere, from anyone. Poetry 101. They can, if they choose, later on in life, read that in a book.

I have my eyes and heart set on the bigger things, on the larger issues, on the other side of the poem.

Not the technical, but the spiritual.

I see the spirit, the spiritual, as being directly linked to the surreal, to the dreamier side of things.

To imagine.

"Imagine there's no Heaven."

John Lennon.

To question.

"Why hast thou forsaken me?"

Christ on the cross.

The rising up.

The miracle of that moment.

That poem.

I want them to learn to see what others fail to see.

I want them to learn to feel what others fail to feel.

I want them to see themselves as being large in this life, as being larger than this life.

I want them to be like Whitman was when he wrote the words, when he made the claim, *I am large. I contain multitudes.*

I also want them to know what beauty is, what beautiful is: to see the beauty, too, not just in the flower as it is blossoming, but to see the beauty, too, in the aftermath, in the flower that has lost its petals.

I want them to see, too, that there are other things in this world, besides flowers, that are just as beautiful.

To see that, yes, a sunrise, a sunset, is beautiful, but so is a sky thickened gray with rainclouds.

To see the beauty in the wrinkled face of an old man.

To see the beauty in a pile of broken glass:

"the back wings / of the / hospital where / nothing / will grow lie / cinders / in which shine / the broken / pieces of a green / bottle."

William Carlos Williams.

So I go in the next week armed not with Kafka, but equipped, instead, with a tin of rubber cement.

I walk in with a blob of rubber cement cold and wet in the palm of my hand.

The first thing I do when I walk into the room, I sneeze.

I raise my hands up to my face.

When I lower my hands, I look down into them to find a handful of what looks a lot like snot.

Boogers.

I tell them that Mr. Pete has a bad cold this morning.

I show them what's in my hands.

A chorus cry of "ohhs" and "oh gross."

I act like I don't know what to do with what's in my hands.

I pick up a piece of construction paper and I use this paper to wipe off my hands.

I hold up this piece of paper so that everyone can see what it looks like now that it has a blob of snot wiped off on it.

It looks like what it is: a blob of snot.

This is not something beautiful for us to look at.

I ask the kids to come up with some words that mean the opposite of beautiful.

Ugly, unbeautiful, yucky, slimy, sick, disturbing.

You get the picture.

Coincidentally, the vocabulary word of the day is anything but unbeautiful.

It is a shimmering word: a word that shimmers even when you say it.

The word is "shimmering."

It's written on the marker board in red magic marker.

S-H-I-M-M-E-R-I-N-G.

As luck would have it, I have with me, in my bookbag, two bottles of silver and gold glitter.

Glitter is shimmering.

Gold and silver are colors that shimmer.

I take this glitter and I sprinkle these bits of silver and gold onto the piece of construction paper that is covered with what looks to be my snot.

The glitter sticks to it as if the snot is glue.

It is glue.

Rubber cement.

I hold this piece of paper up for all eyes to see.

Flakes of silver and gold fall to the floor like shimmering flakes of snow.

I wish you could hear the "oohs" and "ahhs."

"That's beautiful," one girl says.

"That's shimmering," says another.

The snot, the unbeautiful, has been transformed into something beautiful.

Like magic.

I turn the piece of paper sideways and longways to get the students to see whatever it is that they are going to see when I ask them to tell me what you see.

"It looks to me like a silver and gold fish," I say.

I show them what I see and where I see it.

I show them the outline of the fish's gold and silver body.

The fin, the tail, the head, its eye.

I point until they, too, see what I see.

"Now it's your turn," I tell them. "I want you to see something else beautiful here on this piece of paper."

I turn the paper upside down so that the fish that I saw disappears. It becomes something else.

"I see a sun that is shining," says one boy.

Says someone else, "I see a silver and gold football flying through the air."

Yet another says, "It looks like fire."

"Good," I tell them. "You're seeing things my eyes did not see. Thank you for letting me see through your eyes."

I add, "It's your words, it's the power of words, that allow me to look at this picture, to look at the world, through your eyes."

I reach back into my bookbag. Pull out my tin of rubber cement. I tell them that this is what my snot was.

I tell them, "It wasn't really snot."

I confess, "Mr. Pete doesn't really have a cold."

Sometimes we have to break the illusion to make a point.

"Who's the paper captains?" I say.

Two hands raise up.

"Pass out a piece of that construction paper to everyone in this room."

I go around the room, with my tin of rubber snotty-looking cement, and I wipe a blob of it on every piece of paper.

Several students pretend that they've just sneezed out a noseful of snot.

"Bless you," I tell them.

Then I go around the room and I sprinkle bits of silver and gold glitter onto every piece of paper.

The transformation from ugly to beautiful is beginning to take place.

"Tell me," I tell them, "what you see."

I tell them, "Tell me what is beautiful."

I write up on the marker board: "Beautiful is…"

I tell them, "Finish this sentence."

This is the beauty that these beautiful eyes see:

Beautiful is a rainbow in the rain.

Beautiful is a gold star falling from the sky.

Beautiful is a magic glittery bathtub with shiny bubbles coming out of it. The bathtub's power is it can turn people into frogs.

Beautiful is a gold and silver motorcycle with no wheels but it has wings and it is flying to New York City to see the fashion.

Beautiful is a silver monkey swinging on a gold branch. His baby is swinging on a gold branch too. And the baby is as gold as the sun.

Beautiful is the man in the gold hat.

Beautiful is a man on a boat trying to save his people.

Beautiful is a gold and silver car going fast with flames.

Beautiful is a shimmering butterfly flying across a blue sky.

Beautiful is a reindeer pulling a sled and in the sled is a bag of presents and the reindeer is shining in the sky and the bag is glittery.

Beautiful is a beautiful octopus looking for some gold.

Beautiful is a fish doing shimmering tricks in the shimmering gold pond looking for gold.

Beautiful is a gold fairy dancing across the room.

Beautiful is a silver crab going to school in the snow.

Beautiful is a shiny arrow with seahorses helping the arrow to catch a thief.

Beautiful is a sparkly bumblebee that likes strawberry honey. It is eating some right now. It likes to fly but it doesn't like to sting people. Because it is a kind bumblebee that likes to eat strawberry honey.

Beautiful is a yellow bird waking up the sun with his singing.

Beautiful is a firefly going to a schoolhouse to learn how to fly.

Beautiful is a shiny horse with metal wings and the rain is coming down. The rain is made out of gold and silver change.

Beautiful is a star glowing. Beautiful is a glowing star.

Beautiful is a silver and gold star coming out of a spaceship. The star was going to school to learn how to shine.

Like stars, we go to school to learn.

To learn what?

Reading, writing, arithmetic?

The difference between a noun and a verb?

Subject vs. predicate?

Long division?

How to carry the one?

To borrow in order to subtract?

What a compound word is?

The five-paragraph essay?

The words to the Pledge of Allegiance?

How to stand in a straight line?

Get along with others?

To remember "i" before "e" except after "c"?

Synonyms? Antonyms?

Adjectives? Adverbs?

What a metaphor is? A simile?

What are the Ten Commandments?

The words to the Constitution?

That "cat" rhymes with "hat"?

To learn how to shine?

Shine?

Yes, to learn how to shine.

Caged Brains

To LEARN HOW TO see, to see what's not there, to see beyond the surface, to see what nobody else has seen.

That, too, is what and why we go to school to learn.

That is what I teach for, teach toward.

To get the students to shine and to see.

To help me do this, to help the students shine and see, I turn off the lights.

I pull down the shades.

I flip the switch on my slide projector.

A picture emerges out of this darkness and lights up the room.

"Tell me what you see," I tell the students.

"I see a birdcage filled with rope," the first student to speak, to say what he sees, says.

"Okay," I say. "Good. Anyone else see anything different?"

One girl says, "I see a birdcage filled with spaghetti."

The boy sitting next to her says, "It looks like a bunch of worms."

"Thank you," I say. "Good job." Then, "Anyone else? Does anyone see anything else?"

No one says anything.

"So," I say, "does everyone agree that this is a birdcage that we're looking up at projected onto the movie screen?"

All heads nod yes.

"Okay," I say. "Let's warm up our brains a bit by telling Mr. Pete some words that you would use to describe this birdcage."

Here are a few of the words—adjectives—they say: busted, dirty-looking, rusty, broken, old, moldy, junky.

"It looks like something someone threw away," one boy adds when it seems as if we have run out of words.

"That's very insightful," I tell him. "Do you know what I mean when I say 'insightful'?"

He shakes head.

"It means," I tell him, "that what you just said about this birdcage looking like something that someone threw away, it's almost as if you know something about this birdcage that nobody else in this room knows."

He nods with this blessing of knowing.

"Want to know why I say this?" I go on. "Because one thing you should know about the artist who made this sculpture is that he often uses things to make his art that other people have thrown away. He's like a scavenger. Do you all know what I mean when I say that word 'scavenger'?"

"Like a bum," one boy says.

"No." I wince. "Not exactly like a bum."

"Like a junk collector?" another boy asks.

"You could say that," I say. "Anyway, the point I want to make here is that he makes art out of things that other people see as being useless. And I happen to think that's pretty cool."

"You mean an artist made that birdcage?" one girl asks.

I explain to them that, no, the artist didn't actually make the birdcage, though he did make a work of art by taking that busted, dirty-looking, rusty, broken, old, moldy, junky birdcage and filling it up with a tangled-up bunch of rope that some of you said looked like spaghetti, others said it looked to you like worms.

Then I must answer the question that I am almost always asked when I bring this slide into the classroom:

"Is it art?"

And what I almost always say to this is, "Do *you* think it's art?"

"It's not very beautiful," one girl points out.

"You're right," I say, "it isn't very beautiful." Then I ask, "Do you think that art has to be something beautiful?"

"I went to the museum last year with my other school," one boy says, "and we saw this statue of a naked man."

The boy laughs when he says this. The whole class, for half a minute or so, gets a case of the giggles.

"Did you think that it was beautiful?" I ask, after the giggles die down.

"It was sick," he says. "I didn't want to look at it."

"Guess what," I say to this. "That's an appropriate response to a work of art. Some art *is* hard to look at."

I add to this, "And other times we might see a work of art that is hard for us to *stop* looking at."

I tell them about the time I stood for close to three hours in front of a self-portrait by Van Gogh because I swore I saw Van Gogh's eyes move. It looked to me like his eyes were following me whenever I tried to walk away.

I tell them about going to see the Jackson Pollock exhibit at the MoMA a few years back and how I left the museum in such a daze that I went for a walk and I got all turned around and I got lost on the subway back to Brooklyn and I ended up at Coney Island so I ate a Nathan's hot dog (two, with onions) and then I rode the Cyclone (the world's oldest roller coaster) and then I got sick and I threw up my dinner and I spent the night on the beach, where I fell asleep counting the stars.

I tell them, too, about an exhibit I saw last August at the American Folk Art Museum that featured the childlike paintings of a missionary artist by the name of Sister Gertrude Morgan and how Sister Gertrude Morgan's paintings, most of which are paintings inspired by scripture, it was as if Sister Gertrude Morgan's paintings had transformed that museum into a church and how I swear to this day that I could hear the voice of God talking to me as I looked at Sister Gertrude Morgan's beautiful paintings, and what that voice said to me was, simply, "Look closer."

After I tell the students these three stories about my experience of looking at art, I tell them to "look closer" at this birdcage filled with rope.

I tell them that most works of art have titles to go along with them, to help us see what the artist wants us to see.

"The title," I tell them, "shapes how we look at what we're looking at. That's the power of words," I say.

So I ask them to come up with some possible titles for the work of art that we're looking at.

Most of them come up with titles such as "Cage of Rope" or "Cage of Worms."

One boy calls it "Birdcage Without a Bird In It," which I like a lot. I want to write a poem with that as its title.

Another calls it "Cage of Dreams," which I like too because it isn't quite so literal: it goes beyond the actual.

Yet another gives it the title "Cage of Brains."

When I ask him where did he come up with that title, he tells me that the rope looks like a brain.

"Interesting," I tell him.

Then I tell them the actual title, given by the artist himself, a Detroit artist by the name of Tyree Guyton.

"Caged Brain," I tell them.

"I was close," says the boy who came up with "Cage of Brains."

"You win the prize," I say.

"What do I win?"

I lift up my hands to give him some skin, a double high-five. He doesn't leave me hanging, though he does look a bit disappointed that the prize isn't something more than what I've got to give him.

"I want everyone to look closely at this work of art, 'Caged Brain,' and I want you to look at it, and as you look at it I want you to whisper to yourself the words 'Caged Brain' over and over."

"Caged Brain, Caged Brain, Caged Brain."

Next I tell them to look up at Mr. Pete.

I hit the lights, flick off the switch to the slide projector.

"Where is my brain?" is the question I ask.

"In your head," they all agree.

"How do you know this?" I ask next. "You can't see it, can you?"

"But we know," is what they all believe. "Everybody knows that our brain is in our head."

"Fair enough," I say back. "Now answer me this: when you look at Mr. Pete, when you look at my head where my brains are, what do you see?"

They say they see my head, my hair.

"What about my face?" I say. "Isn't my face a part of my head?"

"Yes."

"When you look at my face, what do you see?"

They tell me my eyes, my nose, my cheeks, my lips.

"Okay," I say, "good. Now," I tell them, and I kill the lights.

I turn the slide projector back on.

"Caged Brain" reappears up on the screen.

Like magic.

"Now, if this sculpture is titled 'Caged Brain,' what are we actually looking at? Is it just a birdcage filled with rope anymore?"

"It's a brain," one boy says.

"And our brains are where?" I ask again.

"In our head."

"And when we look at a head, what do we see?"

"A face."

"I see a face," one girl screams out.

"I see eyes," she says, "and a nose, and a mouth with a tongue sticking out of it."

I tell her to come up to the front of the room to point to what she is seeing. I hand her the teacher's yardstick. (Yes, there is actually a yardstick on the ledge of the marker board, to be used for just such a purpose: to point to, to point at, to point out. To get others to see what we want them to see.)

"I see ears," someone else says.

So I hand him the yardstick.

"I see another eye too," says another voice. "And I see a tongue."

Little by little, a face emerges out of the tangled mess of rope that is on the inside of this broken-down, castoff birdcage with no bird inside it.

Again, I remind them (I am reminded) of the power of words: the fact that those two little words, "caged" and "brain," used together as a title, "Caged Brain," taught us to look beyond the surface.

Taught us to look beyond the limits of "birdcage" and "rope."

Taught us to see so much more.

And we, the viewer, and the objects themselves—in the process of looking, in the process of being looked at—

We are transformed.

I ask the students to think about this:

"If your brain is caged, is that a good thing or a bad thing?"

Nearly all agree that a caged brain is a bad brain.

The sole exception to this is a student who thinks of the word "caged" as being a form of protection.

"Like a helmet," he tells me.

Who am I to disagree with that?

We go on.

"If your brain is caged," I say, "what's so wrong, if something is wrong, with a brain that is caged?"

"It can't be free," says one boy.

Says another, "It can't do what it wants."

"It can't think for itself."

"It can't dream."

"Who in this room," I say, "has a brain that is caged?"

No hands raise up.

"That's right," I tell them. "We are all free in this room to think whatever we want. And to dream whatever we want. To do what we want."

I say, with my fist raised up, "My brain isn't caged!"

I say, "Say it with me. My brain isn't caged! My brain is a free brain! My brain is a brain that can think for itself!"

My brain isn't caged!

My brain is a free brain!

My brain is a brain that can think for itself!

"My brain," I say, "is a bird that can fly up to the moon."

"My brain," I say, "is a moon that is always full."

"My brain," I say, "is a fish that can swim out of water."

I ask them, "Who wants to tell Mr. Pete something about your brain?"

I write up on the marker board, "My brain is a _____ that..."

This is some of what they say:

My brain is a bird that walks away when other birds want to fight.

My brain is a bookbag that likes to go to school.

My brain is my imaginary friend that talks to me at night.

My brain is a birdcage with a bird singing in it.

My brain is a pencil that can fly.

My brain is a diamond that shines.

My brain is a book that has all the answers.

My brain is a house with a front door that is always open.

My brain is a flower that never stops growing.

My brain is a tree that never loses its leaves.

My brain is a lightbulb that never burns out.

My brain is a computer that is always turned on.

My brain is a GameCube that I can't stop playing.

My brain is a camera that takes pictures of what I see.

*

You probably remember the TV commercial: *This is your brain.* A man holds up to the camera an egg. *This is your brain on drugs.* He takes the egg and breaks it into a frying pan. The egg begins to sizzle.

Say no to drugs.

But what if that same egg were to become a moon?

Or a baseball?

What if, out of that egg, a rainbow were to arc across the sky?

Or what if a snowflake, or a white bird that was made out of snowflakes, were to rise up?

What if that egg were to break into blossom, like a flower, or like a man watching horses grazing on the side of the highway?

What if that egg was more than just an egg with just an egg inside it?

What if, the next time you cracked open an egg to fry it, the crack of the shell was actually the first note in a song?

No, this is not your brain on drugs.

This is your brain on poetry.

To think outside the shell.

To break open an egg and to see that there doesn't have to be just an egg or a chicken inside it.

Or to put it another way: to look up at the sky and to realize that the sky is more than just the sky.

To stand up on our tippy toes. To reach up with our hand till we break on through to the other side of blue.

Beyond the Blue of the Sky

IT'S TRUE, THE SKY is blue. But I wish I knew a word that could truly describe the blue that is the sky.

Where, I sometimes wonder, does the sky begin? And what, I ask you this, is beyond the blue of the sky?

These are just a few of the problems that the sky raises in those moments when it is most quiet.

Here's a story.

I was nine. It was summer. I was hanging out down by the river, skipping stones out into the river, digging with a stick in the mud at the edge of the river, when I heard what I heard.

What I heard was this:

"Over here."

I turned around. There was nobody there. So I turned back to the river. I went back to me digging in the mud.

"Over here."

I turned around again. I looked again. I didn't see nothing, just a tree. So I went and looked behind the tree. There was no one hiding behind it.

Back to the river.

Back to the mud.

"Up here."

This time I looked up. I did not turn around. The voice, the sound, it was coming from the sky.

The sky was blue.

There was not a cloud in the sky.

It was one of those days.

Not even a bird flying across the blue of the sky to make the sky any other color but blue.

"Up here."

Was it the blue sky talking?

Was it the voice of God calling down to me?

I didn't know.

I was nine.

It was summer.

That was enough for me.

"You wanna come see?" the voice then asked.

I was looking up. All I could see, like I said, was blue.

"See what?" I said.

"See," the voice said, "what's up beyond the blue?"

I shook my head. I didn't really want to see it. I didn't really care about the blue of the sky.

I was nine.

It was summer.

That was more than enough for me.

I looked back down at the river. I looked back down at the mud. Then I looked back up at the sky.

I was nine.

It was summer.

Sometimes I changed my mind.

"Okay," I said. "I'll come see."

"Close your eyes," the voice in the sky told me.

I did what this voice said.

I closed my eyes.

"Tell me what you see."

"I don't see nothing," I said. "I've got my eyes closed."

"Look up," the voice told me.

So I looked up.

"Keep your eyes closed," the voice said. "Now tell me what you see."

I could feel the sun on my face. The sun's light made its way through my eyelids so that I saw a light that was a mixture of yellow and white.

But the blue of the sky I could not see.

I told the voice in the sky what I saw but it wasn't good enough.

"You're gonna have to come up here to see what I want you to see," it said.

The way that it said what it said, I could picture it shaking its head.

"Up where?" I asked.

"Up here in the sky," the voice answered. "Up here beyond the blue of the sky."

Was I dreaming?

Was my imagination, as my mother sometimes liked to say, running amok?

I opened up my eyes.

The sky, I could see it, it was a long way away. Even back then, I wasn't sure where the sky began. But I knew there was no ladder big enough for me to climb up beyond the blue of the sky.

So I told it. I said, "How am I supposed to get up there?"

"Everything that you need," the voice told me, "is right there with you, but I cannot tell you what it is."

I looked around. I didn't see anything that would help me get up to see what was beyond the blue of the sky.

There was no tree big enough.

The river was not a trampoline for me to jump up and down on.

When I jumped up, there was this thing called gravity that we learned about in school that year that pulled me back down.

"Look," the voice said, "inside your pocket."

My pocket?

What was in my pocket?

How could what was in my pocket help me get up to see what was beyond the blue of the sky?

I reached my hand into my pocket.

I pulled out these three things:

1) a wad of pocket lint
2) thirty-three cents in change: two dimes, two nickels, three pennies
3) a pencil

The wad of pocket lint, I threw it up into the air and watched the wind blow it away into the river.

Thirty-three cents, back in 1975, could buy you a medium-sized Slurpee at 7-Eleven, or a pack of Topps baseball cards, or a Snickers candy bar with change to spare. This was back in the day when penny candy actually cost a penny, back in a time when a penny found could give you more than just good luck.

But it wasn't money enough to buy me an airplane, or a ticket on an airplane, so I put the pocket change back into my pocket. I figured I'd save it for a rainy day.

Did I tell you that there were no clouds in sight: that it was one of those blue-sky summer days?

So that left only one thing left from my pocket.

The pencil.

I do not know why I had a pencil in my pocket.

I wasn't a poet.

I didn't carry a pencil around with me so I could write poems the way I carry a pencil around with me now.

I didn't write poems back when I was nine. Actually, I did write a poem back when I was nine. It was a poem about a cloud. No, it was actually a poem written from the point of view of a cloud.

I am a cloud is how the poem began.

> *I am a cloud floating in the blue sky.*
> *I can see the tops of trees.*
> *I can hear the flapping of birds' wings.*
> *I can touch the sun.*

But I wasn't the type of kid who walked around writing poems just for fun.

For fun I was the type of kid who played baseball and liked to play with green army men and liked to dig in the dirt and liked to shoot his BB gun at beer cans and when I was bored I sometimes liked to go down to the river. But not because the river inspired me to write poems.

I liked the river because it was quiet down there and it was a place that I could go to be by myself.

I'd go down to the river when I didn't know where else to go.

I'd go down to the river just to be.

Now that I think about it, even though I didn't write poems about the river when I went down to the river, the part of me that drew me to the river, the part of me that got me to get on my bike and pedal all the way across town to where the river was, that's the part of me that would later on in my life become the poet. That's the part of me that would grow up to be Mr. Pete.

So I held up that pencil. But how would this pencil help me get up to beyond the blue of the sky?

I said so out loud.

I said, to the voice in the sky, "All I've got left is this pencil."

Then I asked, "How is this pencil going to help me get up to beyond the blue of the sky?"

I was about to find out.

The voice in the sky told me how.

The voice said, "Hold your pencil up to your eye."

Then it said, "Look inside."

It told me to tell it, "What do you see?"

"I don't see anything," I told it. "How am I supposed to see inside a pencil?"

The voice in the sky told me to imagine that the pencil in my hand was actually a telescope, that the eraser at the end of it was actually a window and that I could see anything I wanted to see.

"What," the voice asked me, "do you want to see?"

"I guess I want to see what's up beyond the blue of the sky," I said.

"Good," the voice said. "So, look inside. See what's up beyond the blue of the sky."

I looked and I looked but I still could not see what I wanted to see.

In my eyes, a pencil was just a pencil.

"You've got to believe," the voice in the sky told me. "You've got to believe before you can see."

"Believe what?" I asked it—the voice, the sky, the blue of the sky, whoever I was talking to.

"Believe," the voice told me, "that anything is possible."

"But I can't fly," I said. "I'm not a bird."

But the voice in the sky did not agree. We did not see eye to eye.

"If you want to fly," the voice in the sky told me, "then you can fly. If you want to walk across that river, then you can walk across that river. The only thing stopping you from doing so is you."

I gave it some thought. I figured I'd give it a try. But when I flapped my arms like a bird, I did not fly like a bird. When I walked out into the river, the river rose up past my ankles. It did not hold me up.

"Look up," the voice in the sky told me. "Do you want to come up here or not?"

I said that I did.

What could it hurt? Summer was already halfway over. Most of my friends were away on vacation.

What else did I have to do? Where else did I have to go?

"Hold up your pencil," the voice told me. "Hold your pencil up toward the sky and close your eyes."

I did what it told.

"The pencil in your hand," the voice then told me, "it's no longer just a pencil. Now it is a ladder."

"Climb," the voice told me. "Climb on up."

I was afraid of heights, but I did what the voice said. I climbed up.

The pencil wasn't *just* a pencil.

The pencil was a ladder.

It was a ladder big enough to take me all the way up beyond the blue of the sky.

I climbed.

I climbed some more.

"Good," the voice in the sky told me. "You're almost there."

I climbed until I was red in the face.

I climbed until my arms and legs started to hurt.

"Now open your eyes," I heard the voice say.

So I opened my eyes.

I saw the sky.

The sky was bigger than the sky.

The sky was more than just the sky.

The blue of the sky was more than just the color blue.

I wish I could find a word that would describe to you the blue that is the blue of the sky.

And the voice in the sky?

Who did that voice belong to?

Was it the voice of God?

Would you believe me if I told you that it was?

Would you believe me if I told you that that voice was the blue of the sky?

What would you say if I told you that it wasn't the voice of God?

What would you say if I told you that it wasn't the voice of the blue of the sky?

What would you say if I told you that that voice was the voice of an egg, and when I lifted it up, when I held it up to the blue of the sky, when I broke this egg against the sky's bluest edge, there was nothing inside it?

It was just a voice.

It was just a sound.

It was just the sound of my own voice inside my own head.

My Pencil Is

MY PENCIL IS A beat-up pencil. My pencil is a pencil with a nub of a gnawed-down lead. I never stick my pencil into or anywhere near a pencil sharpener. Pencil sharpeners tend to chew and eat pencils like my pencil. I don't want my pencil to be chewed and eaten up. It's true, too, that my pencil, it doesn't have an eraser. The eraser has been erased away. My pencil looks more like a busted-off twig than it does a pencil. It looks like a dog once mistook it for a bone. It has been broken in half, more than once, and has been wood-glued and Scotch-taped and super-glued back together. A Band-Aid now holds the two broken halves together. Once upon a time ago, my pencil, like yours, was a bright and cheerful school-bus yellow. Now it is a plain wood brown.

Let me tell you one more thing about this pencil. This pencil, I wouldn't trade it for any other pencil in the whole wide world. It is mine. My magic pencil. It lets me see things that nobody else can see.

My pencil is a ladder that I climb up it till I get all the way up to where I can see beyond the blue of the sky.

My pencil is the blue-blue sky on a black-black night.

My pencil is a fishing pole that lets me fish for stars.

My pencil is a bird that never stops singing.

My pencil is a shovel, it is a stick of dynamite, a beam of light, a raindrop. It is a big blue Cadillac that never runs out of gas.

In other words:

"Your pencil," I tell the kids, "is more than just a pencil."

It can be anything you want it to be.

It can take you anywhere you'd like it to take you: to Paris, Mars, the moon, the stars, or into your own heart.

It can even take you, just like it took me, beyond the blue of the sky.

"Your pencil," I go on, in praise of—an ode to—the pencil, "can make you into whatever you want to be."

Here again, I'm talking about the transformative power—there's that word again!—of the word, the transcendent possibilities of the brain when it's a bird uncaged: the invitation and the opportunity for us to become other than ourselves.

"Step right up," I say, "into the spotlight."

Here's your chance to cast a shadow that is bigger than the body.

To see and to realize that we are like seashells that wash up on the sea's shore: that when you lift the shell up to your ear you can hear the whole of the ocean, the enormity of that, roaring inside.

"Tell me," I tell the students, "take Mr. Pete inside," I say, "into the magical world of your magic pencils."

My pencil is a ballerina that is spinning around and around.

My pencil is a star so I can make wishes whenever I want.

My pencil is a map so I can go wherever I want.

My pencil is my heart. I can listen to my heart.

My pencil is a rainbow fish that can never be eaten by sharks.

My pencil is a beautiful rose. Every time I smell it, it makes beautiful jazz.

My pencil is a flower swaying in the breeze.

My pencil is a boomerang that you can throw into space.

My pencil is an orange, red, and black camera that can take a picture if you're one million miles away.

My pencil is a pink flower that is a hundred yards tall and it can never be cut down.

My pencil is a red Corvette burning rubber in the sky.

My pencil is a pencil that sings.

My pencil is a flower that keeps on growing until it reaches God's feet.

My pencil is a tiger with sharp teeth that likes to eat people who are mean.

My pencil is a cat with nails that scratch.

My pencil is a dog with black paws that turns into a cat whenever I clap.

My pencil is a flower with red petals dancing in the wind.

My pencil is a rose on a rocket ship.

My pencil is a thousand jelly donuts jumping out of my mouth.

My pencil is a car. It is a good car. It drives me home.

My pencil is a car with shiny wheels that drives over the moon.

My pencil is a castle in the sky with pink flower doors.

A Knock at the Door

I ALWAYS TELL MY students that if there's a knock at the door, be sure to answer it. Be sure to open that door up.

Invite whoever is doing the knocking into your house, into your castle.

Remember what Hafiz said: *"Our words become the house we live in."*

If you don't answer and open the door, there is no story.

There is no poem.

The big bad wolf needs a house for him to blow it, with a huff and a puff, all the way down to the ground.

A door is a thing of great mystery. You never know who or what'll be waiting there on the door's other side.

It was William Blake who said it best:

"If the doors of perception were cleansed," Blake wrote, *"everything would appear to man as it is—infinite."*

Yes, that's what I'm hoping to get at, that's what I want these students to reach for, a place that is beyond themselves.

A place that is infinite.

*

When I open the door, I enter a house that has handprints all over the walls and footprints across the ceiling.

When I open the door, I walk into a world where everyone is dancing to music only they can hear.

When I open the door, I see a stairway made out of light that leads me up to a sky where all the stars know my name.

When I open the door and look inside, I see a house with a little boy sitting on the porch blowing bubbles.

When I open the door, I walk into a room with a window that, when I look through it, I see inside my heart.

Open the door, I tell the students.

Walk, look, inside.

Where are you?

What are you?

Take me by the hand.

By the eyes.

Let me see inside.

I tell the students to close their eyes.

Picture a door. It could be a wooden door, a steel door, a door made out of marshmallows. As long as it's a door they're picturing, a door with a doorknob for them to reach out to and turn.

"Turn the knob," I tell them. "Push open the door."

Picture a room full of second graders, with their eyes closed, with their hands reaching out toward something that isn't there.

Like this, the door opens.

Everything appears as it is.

Infinite.

Mysterious.

Open-ended.

When I open the door, there is a chair sitting in the middle of this room with my shadow sitting in it.

When I open the door, there is a window with a hungry bird singing for food.

When I open the door, I see a rainbow inside and a fish tank full of fish.

When I open the door, I see people dancing and singing.

When I open the door, I see Mr. Pete teaching to all of the classes in the world.

When I open the door, I see my mother in bed reading me a book.

When I open the door, I see my mother crying because she does not want to die when she gets old and I do not either but I know she is going to die even my dad is and it is going to be sad.

The end.

But really it is only the beginning.

Accidents Will Happen

SOMETIMES, THE DOOR OPENS up not so much to a place, to some room inside a house, as it does to a *time* in the young poet's life.

When I was five, something bad happened. I'm seven now, but back when I was five, my mom worked at a job in a big black building. I kept on bugging her that day to let me come to work with her. My mom kept saying no sweetheart, you can't come to work with me because, she said, she had to work. When my mom went to work that day, my mom, she never came back. My brother and me waited until dark time for our mom to come back home. I waited and watched for the car to drive up to drop off my mom. When my neighbor Monique came over, we went inside our house and ate and drank and then I played with my neighbor Miranda until Bookie came over with her white car. We drove in that white car to the church to see my mom. At church, it was blue inside like the sky. Three days later it was Christmas. The bus that hit my mom as she waited at the bus stop—the driver of that bus was drunk. He didn't even know what he did when he ran that bus up against the bus stop bench killing my mom.

So wrote the boy with the blind third eye.

*

I'm not sure how, or why, this poem (titled "Until Dark Time") came about. I did not tell the students to write about a loss. I did not tell them to write about a time when something bad happened. I simply told them that there is a door that needs to be opened, that there is a knock at this door and, like my mother always told me, and like I like to tell my students, if somebody's knocking at the door, the polite (i.e. the right) thing to do is to go to the door and answer it. To hide from the knocking, to pretend that you're not home, that you didn't hear it, that would be a lie (not the kind of a lie that is lying for the sake of making believe, like how we do in a poem or a story).

Maybe it was the word *when* that did the triggering. Or maybe when the door opened, the boy with the blind third eye looked and saw his mother standing there behind it. In the end, it doesn't really matter what triggered the poem. What matters is that the poem was written. What matters is that the boy who wrote this poem (the boy with the blind third eye) made something beautiful and moving out of something bad that did, sadly, tragically, happen. The way I see it, a transfer of power took place through the writing of this poem. Call it another form of poetic transformation. The boy with the blind third eye proved, without a doubt, that he could see. He saw with his heart. He reached down into a place that is more inward than is safe to go. And here, from that place of silence and grief, he returned to us a poem of compassion. And because of this, because this boy dared to do so, the spirit of his mother lives on—through the poem, through the poet. The mother here doesn't have a story unless her boy gives it back to her through the power of his voice.

That's the power, and the beauty, and the necessity, the urgency, the truth, of the written word.

The magic of the pencil.

Nothing Beautiful

ONE TIME, WHEN I was teaching a class at another grade school, I wrote the word "beautiful" on the blackboard.

B-E-A-U-T-I-F-U-L

Then I asked the students to tell me about something beautiful in their lives.

We defined "something beautiful" as something that, when you have it in your life, when you can see it, or hear it, or smell it, or taste it, or touch it (we had just talked about the five senses), that beautiful something makes your heart feel fuller and happier than it does when you don't have it in your life.

We went around the room. The students talked, as you might expect, about flowers and butterflies, about the sun rising and the sun setting, about the moon and the stars shining in the night; they talked about dogs and cats; they talked about video games; they talked about the blue of the sky.

One by one we made a list of things that look beautiful, things that sound beautiful, things that smell beautiful, taste beautiful, feel beautiful.

Rainbows, pianos, my mother's perfume, pizza, the grass sticking up between your toes.

"My reflection when I look in the mirror," one little girl said.

"That's something beautiful," I said to this.

Then I told them, "I hope all of you believe that what she just said is also true for you."

Most heads nodded yes.

I was happy to see this.

I told them that in the eyes of Mr. Pete, there's nothing more beautiful than a room full of second graders gazing into their magic pencils.

"I love the look of that," I said.

Then I told them how much I love the sound, the silence, of a room full of second graders writing poems.

The sound that is made when paper and pencil meet.

"I love the sound of that."

I pulled out a book from my bookbag and told them how much I love the smell of a brand-new book, that I can actually smell and give thanks to the trees that the paper was made from.

"I even love the taste of ink," I told them, "when it runs down from the corners of my mouth."

"Why would you eat ink?" one little boy wanted to know, and rightly so.

"Because," I told them, "*I have been eating poetry. There is no happiness like mine.*"

I told them that "something beautiful" could be a place you like to sometimes go to when you want to be alone.

"Like your bedroom," I said. "Your bedroom could be 'something beautiful.'"

I told them that "something beautiful" could be a place you like to go with friends.

"The park, the playground, Chuckie Cheese," I said.

Something beautiful could be something you like to do.

"Like play basketball, or dance, or ride your bike."

Something beautiful, in essence, could be *anything* beautiful.

And so we went around the room. I wanted each student to have a chance, to have a voice in our celebration of all things beautiful in this world.

All but one student had something beautiful to say.

That one student was a little girl who could not think of something, anything, beautiful in her world.

"What's your favorite food?" I asked her.

I asked her, "What's your favorite song?

"If you could go do anything right now," I said, "what would you go do?

I said, "If you could *be* anywhere right now other than here in this room with Mr. Pete, where would you go?"

She shook her head. "Nowhere," she said. "Nothing," she added. "Nothing is beautiful to me."

"Nothing beautiful?" I said to this.

I waited for her to say something.

I said this again. "Nothing beautiful?"

"Nothing," she said, "is beautiful."

"*You're* beautiful," I told her.

"No, I'm not."

She looked away.

"Isn't Mr. Pete something beautiful?" I asked her. "I try my best to make your heart feel happy when I'm in your classroom with you."

She didn't say anything to this.

This little girl who I will call Nothing Beautiful was a closed-up flower that was not about to open up.

Somewhere, I was sure, the sun was shining.

Maybe just not in this room right now.

But I had faith that someday, somewhere, this little girl would see the light and would see the world as a beautiful place.

"Would you do Mr. Pete a big, big favor?" I asked her, before the bell was about to ring to end the day.

She looked up at me, looking more than just a little wilted.

"I'll be back a week from today," I told her. "What I'd like you to do," I said, "is for you to go around your neighborhood, talk to all the people you know, your mother, your father, your grandma and grandpa, aunts and uncles. Ask whoever you want (but don't talk to strangers), ask them the question: 'What's something beautiful in your life?' Do you think you could do that for Mr. Pete?"

She nodded her head yes.

This, I knew, was at least a start.

Every flower is born and born to bloom.

I tried not to think too much about Nothing Beautiful after I left the school, but it was hard not to think about her. How was it possible that a little girl, eight years old, felt that there was nothing beautiful in her world? It's true that many of the students I work with live in neighborhoods that are less than beautiful: burned-down and run-down houses, trash, castoff furniture, boxes of old toys, heaped in piles at the side of the curb, sometimes in the middle of the street, waiting for weeks to be picked up—broken glass on the sidewalks, playgrounds with swings that have no seats. You get the picture. You've heard it before, seen it before, I'm sure. I'm not telling you anything new or eye-opening when I tell you that it's a difficult reality that these kids have to face. And sometimes, I'm sure—how could it not?—this hard reality shapes the way that they see.

But back at home, every time I did think of Nothing Beautiful, when I told my wife about her, I kept picturing a flower: a flower that had been stepped on before it had the chance to break into blossom.

But then I remembered something my wife once said to me. What she said was, and I don't remember the context for her saying it, but she said it nonetheless. "Even crushed violets smell beautiful."

This, I knew, was true.

And I hoped this would be true, too, for Nothing Beautiful.

When I came back a week later, that little girl, Nothing Beautiful, she came running up to me in the hall.

"Mr. Pete," she said. "I did the homework. I asked them what you asked me to ask about something beautiful."

Was this the same little girl who said, just a week ago, "Nothing is beautiful to me"?

"That's good news," I said. "Thank you."

"Guess what my mama said was something beautiful to her?" she said.

When she looked at me, she looked at me with eyes that were like moons that could light up the whole sky.

I was almost blinded by happiness.

I have been eating poetry. There is no happiness like mine.

"What?" I said. "What did she say?"

She said, "Me."

She said, tugging at my shirtsleeve, "She said that I was something beautiful."

She said, "My mama told me I was more beautiful than the most beautiful flower."

She held me by the hand.

I was held.

I am still being held by this moment.

There was a light, I swear, that seemed to be radiating out from that place on her forehead where I like to tell students that this is where your third eye is, smack dab in the middle of your head.

"That," I said, "is a beautiful thing for your mother to say."

The light had hit her and now it was shining back out.

"I wrote a poem about it too," she told me.

"You did," I said. "Can I see it?"

"It's in my locker," she said, "but I've got it with me in my head."

"Let's hear it," I said.

"My mama," she said, "is something beautiful to me," she said. "She is more beautiful than a bee sitting on a flower. My mama says I am more beautiful than the most beautiful flower in the world. I know that my mama is right because my mama don't lie and she likes to sing in the shower."

This flower, this beautiful flower, in a week's time, had fully come into bloom.

Here's a few things you should know about Nothing Beautiful.

Nothing Beautiful doesn't have a daddy. That is, she doesn't know who her daddy is, or where he lives, or if he is alive.

"He could be dead," she tells me.

Then she asks me, "Do you have a dad?"

I tell her that I do.

"He must be old," she says.

Nothing Beautiful does have sisters. Twins. They are both in the first grade.

Nothing Beautiful's two sisters both had the same daddy.

Nothing Beautiful's two sisters both had the same daddy but now their daddy is dead.

"He got shot in the head," Nothing Beautiful tells me when I ask her if her sisters' daddy is nice.

Nothing Beautiful lives at her grandma's house with her two sisters and her mama and her grandma.

I know where this house is.

Believe me when I tell you that you wouldn't want to live in this house.

What can I say about this house?

I could say that it's a rundown house, that the gutter is dangling down off the side of the house, that two of the windows are boarded up with wood, that the porch steps are crumbling, that a tireless car is sitting up on cinderblocks on the side of the house. I could say that the house looks like it's been set on fire (it has). I could tell you that the windows of this house have been shot out (they have). But all of this that I *could* say only tells you a small part of what I see.

What I *feel* about this house is this: that nobody should have to live in a house that looks like this house. Unless you've lived in a house that looks like this house, you cannot know what it is like to live in Nothing Beautiful's house.

Nothing Beautiful's granddaddy doesn't live with them in this house.

Nothing Beautiful's granddaddy doesn't live with them in this house because he lives in a prison where he is serving a life sentence.

When I ask her what did her granddaddy do, she tells me that he shot her sisters' daddy in the head.

"My mama said I'm something beautiful," she tells me.

And what I tell her is, "That's because you are."

Something Beautiful

I GO INTO CLASS armed with a box, a wrapped present, with a red bow on it and ribbon ribbony-curled.

"Who can guess what's inside this box?" I say.

Hands raise high.

"I know."

"I know what it is."

"It's a…"

"No, it's not a video game, it's not a DVD, it's not a Power Ranger or a pack of Pokemon cards," I tell them.

"A magic pencil," one boy guesses.

"No, it's not a magic pencil," I am almost sorry to say.

"What it is then, Mr. Pete?"

The students all want to know.

So I tell them.

Do you want to know?

I'll tell you too.

"It's a poem," I say.

"A poem?"

"Yes, a poem," I say. "Your words," I tell them, "are gifts."

Poetry as a gift.

Poetry *is* a gift.

I tell them that we are going to write poems—love poems—about and for somebody beautiful in our lives.

Our mothers and fathers, brothers and sisters, grandmas and grandpas, aunts and uncles, cousins and friends.

"Remember," I tell them. "Somebody's beautiful not just because they look pretty on the outside. Someone's beautiful," I say, "because when you're with them, they make your heart feel happy on the inside."

I ask them, "Who are you going to give the gift of your words to?"

I point out, "Both Christmas and Kwanzaa are coming up just around the bend. Save yourself some money. Give someone beautiful to you this poem as a gift."

We begin by making a list of things—not people—that are, to us, in our eyes, beautiful things.

Something that is beautiful to see.

Something that is beautiful to hear.

Something that is beautiful to smell.

Something that is beautiful to taste.

Something that is beautiful to touch, to feel.

Then I tell them, "Your someone beautiful is even more beautiful than any of these beautiful things."

We begin with the title: "My Something Beautiful."

Line 1: My _____ is my something beautiful.

Line 2: She/He is more beautiful than _____.

"Fill in the second line's blank," I say, "with something that *looks* beautiful to you."

Here on these lists I see litanies of all sorts of beautiful things: moons, stars, waterfalls, fields of yellow dandelions, a big-screen TV.

My mother is more beautiful than the moon that shines at night.

My brother is more beautiful than God himself.

My sister is more beautiful than the stars twinkling in the sky.

My grandma is more beautiful than fireworks exploding on the Fourth of July.

You get the picture.

We move on.

We keep going.

Line 3: She/He is LIKE the sound of _____.

She is like the sound of the sea.

He is like the sound of a piano.

She is like the sound of beautiful songs sung at Christmas.

He is like the sound of a civil rights speech.

She is like the sound I hear beating inside my heart.

Can you hear the beauty?

The love?

We move on through the senses, moving back and forth between using *like* or saying *more than*.

I talk to them for a bit about the transformative (there's that word again) power of love.

"Love," I tell them, because I believe that it's true, "can change and save the world."

I tell them to let me see: "How powerful is your love for this person? What," I say, "can your love transform?"

Our love is so strong it can transform guns into magic pencils.

Our love is so incredible it can transform dead tigers into alive tigers.

I want them to end with a direct metaphor to really nail the poem home: to really hammer the poem straight into the heart.

I ask them to think about this: "If your someone beautiful was something other than who he or she is, what would that something be? A bird? The moon? A butterfly? A tiger?"

I ask them, "What is your favorite color?"

In the end, we end with lines like these:

She is my beautiful baby-blue flower.

He is my beautiful yellow sun.

Love Is a Big Blue Cadillac

So POETRY IS A gift.

Poetry as a gift.

Of love.

"But what," I ask the students, "is love?"

I tell them that I'm thirty-nine years old and I'm not sure if I know what love is.

"Love," one girl tells me, "is when you love somebody."

"But what does that mean, 'when you love somebody,' exactly?" I ask her.

"It means," she tells me, "that you'd do anything for them."

"Okay." I nod my head. I suppose I know something about the kind of love she is talking about: sacrifice and compromise in the name of love.

Another student says, "It means that when they're with you, you feel safe."

"Love makes you happy," says another girl, who is missing her two top front teeth. When she says that word, "love," it almost sounds as if she is saying "laugh," which I suppose laughter is linked with love.

So we move around the room, a room full of second graders talking about love. I can think of worse ways to spend my day. But I still haven't really learned anything new about love. If there's one thing I'm always looking for from the kids, from any writer, it's a way of saying something new.

One of my mottos is, "Already said, already dead."

I want them to find a new way into old subjects. I want them to find a new way of saying what their child hearts and eyes understand and know.

So we pick up where we last left off with the last lines of our "My Somebody Beautiful" poems.

The power of metaphor.

Forget *like* or *as.*

Tell me, I tell the students, what love is.

Again, we make use of our favorite colors.

Then I ask them, "What is some*thing*, not someone, that you love? You might love the way it looks, or the way it sounds, or the way it smells. Anything," I tell them, "can be turned, can be transformed"—there's that magic word again!—"into a metaphor."

I tell them to take a look around the room. Look outside the window. We are surrounded, I say, by metaphors.

Metaphors waiting to be made.

Whenever I talk about metaphors, I can't help but think of that scene in the film *Il Postino* where Pablo Neruda and Mario, the postman, are sitting by the sea and Neruda recites one of his poems in praise of the sea.

> *Here on the island, the sea, so much sea. It spills over from time to time. It says yes, then no. Then no. In blue, in foam, in a gallop, it says no, then no. It cannot be still. My name*

is sea, it repeats, striking a stone but not convincing it.
Then with the seven green tongues of seven green tigers of
seven green seas it caresses it, kisses it, wets it, and pounds
on its chest, repeating its own name.

"Well?" Neruda asks.

In other words, what do you think of my poem?

The postman gazes back at the poet with the eyes of a child who is, for the first time in his life, seeing the waves of the sea.

"It's weird," the postman tells Neruda.

"What do you mean, weird?" Neruda says back. He gives the postman a look. "You're a severe critic."

"No," the postman explains, "not the poem. Weird, weird, how I felt when you were saying it."

"And how was that?"

"I can't explain it," the postman shrugs.

But then he does just that: he *does* explain it. He finds the words that he is searching for. The words that his heart, his throat, wish his lips could say. And when he does find it, it is like a first kiss.

"I felt like a boat," the postman explains to the poet, "tossing around on those words."

"Do you know what you've just done, Mario?" Neruda asks, pleased by the transformation of his postman-student.

"No, what?"

"You've just invented a metaphor."

Listen, now, to a few of these blackbirds sing with yellow ribbons (metaphor, metaphor!) ribboning out from their mouths.

Love is a blue sky where angels fly in circles making blackbirds sing.

Love is a blue river that turns all the things it touches the color blue.

Love is a red flower that I plant into the ground. At night I can hear it praying.

Love is a red apple growing on a tree waiting for you to eat it.

Love is a blue bird that lays her eggs and waits for them to hatch.

Love is a red moon that sings.

Love is a black girl in a green dress.

Love is a pink heart with a sun inside it.

Love is a white horse that never stops running.

Love is a yellow flower that never dies.

Love is a big blue Cadillac that never runs out of gas.

Love is a big blue Cadillac that never runs out of gas.

Think about that.

This is a love that is everlasting.

A love that, like some hybrid car of the future, fuels itself.

Here's the rest of the poem.

> *Love is a big blue Cadillac*
> *that never runs out of gas.*
> *It drives to Mississippi to see his wife.*
> *I watch them kiss.*
> *The sun rises like a cherry*
> *turning the whole universe red.*

This is a love that will take us wherever we want to go.

Yes, love takes to the road, from Motown to Mississippi—even if, or maybe especially if, it's for a kiss.

This is a love that goes out of its way.

This is a love that, for those who witness a kiss like this, this kiss has the power to transform (that word!) not just the world that's witness to this kiss, but it can change the "whole universe."

That's one powerful metaphor.

The power of a kiss.

Inside My Heart

"LOVE," ONE STUDENT TOLD me when we were talking about love, "is what's inside your heart."

"But if you can't see it," I said, "how do you know it's there?"

"It's there, Mr. Pete," she said back. "You can feel it. You don't need to see it."

Okay, this made sense. So I nodded my head. What I didn't say was that there are people in the world who need to see a thing before they can believe it.

These are the kinds of people who would never be able to see inside a magic pencil.

But it's those kinds of people that inspire me, Mr. Pete, to do what I do the next time I walk into that classroom.

I walk in, again, with a box, but this time the box isn't wrapped up to look like it's a gift.

It's a plain brown box this time—nothing shiny or gift-like about it—the kind of a box that a box of books might come in when it comes in the mail. In fact, that's exactly what kind of box it is. It's the box that came to me in the mail with a boxful of my books, *The Singing Fish*, on the inside of it.

It's a good-sized box. A big enough box to hold a small, thirteen-inch-screen TV. Lots of things could fit inside it.

Again, I ask the students what do they think is inside this box.

There is no shortage of guesses: everything from a boxful of frogs to a boxful of magic pencils to books to candy canes to Beanie Babies to a boxful of brand-new shoes that I'm bringing in to give to the poor.

One boy even guesses that, on the inside of this box, there is a boxed-up (i.e. caged) brain.

"Close," I tell this boy. "You're real close."

"Is it the skull of a skeleton?"

No.

"Is it a bunch of worms?"

No.

"Is it a dead man's head?"

"A dead man's head?" I ask back.

"Like in that poem-story that you read us? Remember, Mr. Pete. The one about the dead man in the bar."

It's true. I do remember. I did read them some of the prose poems by Charles Simic, one poem that begins, *The dead man steps down from the scaffold. He holds his bloody head under his arm.*

"No, it's not a dead man's head," I say. "And no, it's not the bloody thumb that the lady in the black limousine uses as lipstick to paint her lips red." This, too, is an allusion to one of Simic's poems.

Then I ask them, "Do you give up?"

They give up.

What I should say to them is, *Never give up.*

I'll save that lesson for another day.

*

"Tell us what's inside the box!" they say.

"Let us see inside the box!"

So I reach my hand into this box. I make like there's a shark inside this box that's chewing my arm off.

"Help me! Help me! Let go!"

A part of my job, I realize, as a teaching poet in the school, is to make the students laugh. To keep them entertained. Yes, even if it means resorting to cheesy gimmicks like me acting like I am getting attacked by a shark in a box.

Here we are now, entertain us.

So sang Nirvana's Kurt Cobain on one of his better days.

Kids these days.

I stick my arm back in.

"So you're sure you want to know what's inside this box?"

"Tell us, Mr. Pete!"

"So you're sure you want to see what's inside this box?"

"Let us see!"

I fish with my hand around and down inside this box.

If you're thinking that maybe that twelve-legged purple octopus with the goldfish-orange top hat with the green fuzzy feather dangling down off the top of it is hiding here on the inside of this box, think again.

I tell the kids that if they're thinking that maybe that twelve-legged purple octopus with the goldfish-orange top hat with the green fuzzy feather dangling down off the top of it is hiding here on the inside of this box, I tell them too to think again. That octopus, I remind them, lives forever inside my pencil.

This box is not a pencil.

This box, it is my heart.

It is what's inside my heart.

What's inside my heart is on the inside of this box.

I am reaching inside this box to show you my heart.

I tell this to the kids.

Their eyes grow big.

When was the last time someone said they were going to show you his heart?

I am fishing around with my hand on the inside of this box.

I am fishing for my heart.

When I pull my hand up and out from the inside of this box, I am holding in my hand a picture of me, Mr. Pete, holding in my hands a fish.

It is a big fish.

It is a fish that is almost as big as my daughter, who is in this picture standing next to this fish.

"Inside my heart," I say, "there is a fish."

I tell them that. "Inside my heart…" Here my voice begins to trail away, remembering that day when I brought this fish home to show it to my daughter. I remember the look on her face when I held up this fish.

I am forever held by that look on her face. It was a look of complete awe: a look that we look at the world with when we are seeing something—a fish, a flower, a snowflake—for the very first time.

"Inside my heart," I say, and here I fight back the tears that are blurring my eyes, "there's a little girl named Helena."

But that's not all.

I fish my hand back into this box and I pull out another picture: of a little boy riding a bike.

"Inside my heart," I tell them, "there is a little boy named Solomon."

I fish my hand back in and pull out a little silver key, light as a dime.

"This key," I tell the kids, "is my son's bike lock key." Then I tell them, "But it's also a key to my heart."

And that's not all, either.

When I fish my hand back into this box, I pull out a hockey puck, a baseball glove; I pull out a letter, a Post-It note, a business card, a scribbled drawing; I pull out a postcard, a guitar pick, a Pokemon card, a pocket watch; I pull out a bluebird's feather, a pencil, a hospital bracelet, a leaf.

These are just some of the things that I pull out from this box.

This is just some of what is inside my heart.

All these things are things—*nouns*—that, in one way or another, people I love have given to me.

All of these things are—there is no other way for me to say this—they're gifts that have been given to me from the heart.

The heart is a well that will never run dry.

It is a river that will never run out of fish.

Behind every photograph (of a daughter or a son or a fish), behind every object (hockey puck, baseball glove, leaf), there is a memory, there is a story, a poem, waiting to be told, waiting to be made.

"Reclaimed" is a word I like to use.

Waiting, too, to be transformed (there's that word again!) from something that could be easily forgotten, like a fish that gets away, into a thing that you cannot forget: a fish that you put up on a wall.

I remember catching that fish. I remember being out on the ice, late February, with a spear in hand, gazing down into the murky winter waters of the Detroit River. I remember when that fish, like a ghost it appeared, it slowly drifted into the TV screen–like square in the ice that we were fishing through, and I waited and I watched and then I let go of that spear, I gave it a flick with my wrist, and that fish was mine.

And I remember coming home. I remember going into the house and calling out to Helena to come look at this fish.

I remember the look in her eyes when she took a look at that fish.

She had never before seen a fish this big this up close.

Snow was on the ground.

In this picture, she has pink slippers on her feet.

I hold this big fish up beside her.

Even the fish, I swear this to you: even the fish is smiling.

Even though this fish is dead.

Nothing ever dies.

I tell this to the kids.

I tell this to my own kids.

Nothing dies as long as we remember it.

That's what heaven is.

That's where heaven is.

It's in our memory.

In our brains.

It's in our hearts.

Tell this to the mountain. Go tell this to the boy with the blind third eye: a boy whose mother is dead.

I do.

The mountain knows that the dead never really die.

I tell this to the boy with the blind third eye. I tell this to this boy whose mother, I know, is dead.

And what he says is, "I've got nothing inside my heart."

The boy with the blind third eye, I see—I have known this from the very start—he is like Neruda's sea.

It says yes, then no. Then no. In blue, in foam, in a gallop, it says no, then no.

But I, too, am like a different sea: a sea that *repeats, striking a stone,* even though I might not be *convincing it.*

Maybe what I need to do is to do more than just strike a stone. Maybe what I need to do is to go inside the stone itself.

Maybe that's how I can get the stone to see that, like the sea, all that we love never really dies.

On my break, that day, I go down to the cafeteria, I go down to the boiler room, I go to places in this school that I didn't even know existed. I go in search of boxes. I am like a pilgrim looking for what others throw away. Like a pilgrim with a steadfast heart, I have faith that I will find what it is I need.

I scrounge up enough boxes, though some are pretty beat-up and broken down, so that every student gets, is given, a box.

"This box," I tell them, "holds what's inside your heart."

I tell them that, for next week, "I want us all to reach inside our box. We're gonna go fishing inside our hearts."

To show and to tell the world—to tell those with eyes to see and ears to hear—what lives inside their lives.

As I leave I turn and wave and call out the words that every fisherman likes to hear: "Fish on!"

Memory Is a Box

LET ME TELL YOU a bit more about what's inside my box, or what's inside my heart. Let me begin by telling you about the hospital bracelet that is so central to my life. It is so big, I'm surprised it fits inside this box.

I remember when my daughter was born, a nurse took my hand and she snapped a plastic bracelet around my wrist with the words "Baby Girl Markus" written on it in blue ink. Even after we came home from the hospital, I didn't take the bracelet off. I couldn't get myself to cut it off, to take scissors to this thing—this piece of plastic—that connected me in some beautiful way to the rebirth that had occurred to me that day. The last time I had worn one of these bracelets was the day I had been born. I knew that this object, which most people throw away, it was for me a metaphor waiting to be made. It's true that I did take scissors to my daughter's umbilical cord; I could make that cut, an act that I knew was very symbolic. But that bracelet, I kept that strip of plastic on my wrist for thirteen months. I remember the students I was teaching that winter in some of the Detroit high schools, they'd always ask me about the bracelet. I think maybe they thought I had just been released, or maybe had escaped, even, from some psychiatric hospital. They always seemed relieved when I told them that I'd just had a baby.

"When?" I remember one girl wanted to know. When I told her, "December third," she gave me a look, then she said, "No offense, but don't you think it's time to take that thing off?" Okay, so it was mid-April, but like I said, I wasn't yet ready, I wasn't willing, to begin that lifelong process of letting go.

And so I hold onto this bracelet, I keep it here inside this box, so that that day will never be lost, never be forgotten, never be taken away.

This bracelet, this small piece of that day—this ratty-looking strip of faded plastic—it is a piece of my heart.

It is mine.

It is mine to keep.

It is mine to do with it whatever I please.

That's what's so beautiful about memory, about writing from memory: what we remember, how we remember it, it is ours to tell it the way that we remember it. It is our story, our version of the world, according to us.

And no one can take that away.

When a leaf falls from a tree, the world keeps right on spinning. Most of us walk right by it. A leaf falling is just that: a leaf falling.

But for a child, in the eyes of a child, a leaf falling can be a miraculous thing.

Take my son, Solomon, for instance.

I remember the first time he really took notice of the leaves falling in the fall.

He was maybe eighteen months old. It was actually his second fall, but this was the first fall, with the wonderfully dramatic change in colors, with the wind blowing the leaves off the trees, that he could actually take pleasure and wonder in. I could see his mind working behind his blue-sky eyes, wondering why are these leaves falling? Why are these leaves turning from green to yellow to red?

It's a good question.

It's a question that I can't really, with any authority, answer.

I know it has something to do with light.

The amount of light?

The lack of light, maybe?

But that's all I know.

I remember us running around our yard trying to catch the falling leaves. It is not an easy thing to do. You can never tell when a leaf is going to fall. And when it falls, the wind likes to play a game of keep-away.

But my son stuck with it. He stood under enough trees and he stood there long enough looking up to catch a falling leaf falling.

And when he did, he held that yellow leaf to his body. He held that yellow leaf up against his heart.

It was almost as if he was saying, to the leaf, Listen to this.

I am alive.

I am alive.

This is what I want you to see.

See this little boy with this little yellow leaf in his little hand run with this leaf over to his father. See this boy hold this leaf up for his father to take it. "For you, Dada. I catched this leaf for you."

This leaf, like these words, like a poem, it too can be, it can become, it can be transformed (there's that word again) into something other than just a leaf.

Yes, it's true, I've seen it with my own eyes, I hope I've shown it here to you: a leaf falling, a leaf falling, it can be a gift.

But enough about Mr. Pete.

Mr. Pete has a heart that is sentimental down to its core.

I am not apologizing for that.

I am not asking for forgiveness.

What I am doing is, I am simply telling it like it is.

My heart is a box full of pop songs, a box full of love songs, and I am singing them here to you.

Hear my voice.

And then lift your voice even higher.

I tell this to the kids.

Sing, I tell them.

It doesn't matter if you can sing, I say.

All that matters is that you do sing.

You are the music while the music lasts.

This is T.S. Eliot.

And now this is Henry Miller singing about "the song":

> *I am going to sing for you, a little off key perhaps, but I will sing. To sing you must first open your mouth. It is not neces-sary to have an accordion, or a guitar. The essential thing is to want to sing. This then is a song. I am singing.*

"Who," I say, "wants to sing the song, the song that's in—this song that is—your singing heart?"

The Singing Hearts

LISTEN TO THESE HEARTS sing.
> When I open up this box.
> When I fish my hands into my heart.
> I fish out.
> I remember...

...when I was four and I learned how to sing. I remember that when I was in my old school in the lunchroom I was singing a good song. It was called "Amazing Grace."

...the first time I saw a butterfly. It was red and blue and yellow. I called down my whole family to see. My brother tried to kill it.

...the day my baby sister was born. She came home in a pink car seat. I was taking a nap. When I woke up she was sleeping. I was so excited. But a few years later, I was kind of jealous because she was getting all the attention.

...the first time I learned how to ride a bike. I remember it was hard because there were too many rocks. But I finally learned how. I fell a couple of times but I did it.

...when my dog China had puppies. I remember Big Boy got sick. I remember that Speedy was the first to walk. I remember when China ate the other puppy and it was a girl.

...*when I first started skating. I remember that I was at the North-land Roller Rink and I was skating with my baton class. I remember they put little blue bows on our skates. I remember going really fast. I remember holding my mom's hand. She was going real slow. But I was going fast.*

...*when I was a baby and I had a baby blanket and it had Mickey Mouse on it and I remember when I got clothes that were pink and I remember when I got jeans that were blue and I had pajamas that were green.*

...*when my cousins sprayed me with a water gun. I remember when my cousins poured water all over me. I was so wet I walked side to side just like a penguin.*

...*when my teacher Mrs. Boyd turned on the music and the whole class danced and played the limbo.*

...*me and my grandma were playing a Lord of the Rings game and she asked what are the elves doing in the morning and everybody said they were eating breakfast but I said they were just waking up.*

...*when I learned how to skate. I was scared but I tried because my dad said keep trying. I remember falling. And when I fell, I got back up.*

On Growing Up

BEFORE TOO LONG, THESE students—second graders!—they will begin to hear the words that no child should have to hear:

It's time to grow up!

Oh, to be a child.

This book, I hope, is my ode to the child.

Even though the story never goes there, I know in my heart of
hearts that Peter Pan was a poet.

*"Every child at play behaves like an imaginative writer, in that he
creates a world of his own or, more truly, rearranges the things of his
world and orders it in a new way.... It would be incorrect to think that he
does not take this world seriously; on the contrary, he takes his play very
seriously and expends a great deal of emotions on it."*

That's Sigmund Freud doing the talking there.

When I teach writing to adults, when I teach high schoolers, I
always dare them, that first day that we're together, that in order for
them to become a writer on the page, they must become a child again.

Reclaim.

Transform.

Become.

They must, in other words, see the world the way a child sees it.

When the moon rises at night, they must point to it, open-jawed, and say, "Look, there's the moon."

I'll never forget the time, two summers ago, riding on the F-Train back to Brooklyn, when my daughter Helena jumped up from where she was sitting and said, loud enough so that everyone in the car could hear her say it:

"Look, Daddy, look, the moon, the moon!"

The moon was rising big and whole and holy over the scarred skyline of Manhattan, and I swear to you, that night, when Helena sang these words out and pointed with her finger at *moon, moon, look, Daddy, look*—because she knows that I love the moon so much—all heads and eyes turned toward that sound, and there they saw the moon, again, as if they had never before seen it.

To look at the moon, to see the moon, like that night: as if you are seeing it for the very first time.

I say moon is horses in the tempered dark, because horse is the closest I can get to it.

To stand beneath *moon* and gaze up in awe of it.

What if the moon, I say to the students, what if the moon were more than just the moon?

What if the moon was—what?

How would you finish that sentence?

Emerson wrote: "Every word was once a poem."

Maybe the moon was once a poem too.

Maybe the moon is a fish, or a fish eye, or a bird without a voice.

Maybe the moon is a button on an old man's overcoat.

Or a tambourine. A lighthouse. Or the bottom of a bucket.

Oh, how I love that little word, "or."

And the word "maybe" too.

Words of possibility. Words of "what if."

On the marker board I make a circle.

"What is this?"

A circle, yes.

"What else might this be?"

A hula hoop, a snowball, a plate, a basketball rim, a saucer of milk, a blind man's eye.

They are beginning to get the picture.

"What else," I then ask, "might the moon be?"

Here is some of what they see and say:

I think the moon is a brain
or it might be a letter O that lost P
or a football with no strings.

I think the moon is a piece of rice
or a glowing piece of silver
or a wheel on a car.

I think the moon is a donut with no hole
or a clock with no numbers or arms.

I think the moon is a fingernail
or a piece of candy lost in the sky
or a school with no people in it.

I think the moon is a stone frozen in air
or God with no church.

I think the moon is a zero
or a black hole
or a stop sign with no words.

I think the moon is a star with no points
or a house with no roof.

I think the moon is a sunspot
blown off the sun, or maybe

the moon is a lost little boy
who brings light to the night
so other people don't get lost like him.

To do the same, to see always more than, other than, with *flower,*
river, mud.
   Bottle, butterfly, sky.
   They must relearn all over again.
   We must unlearn the constellations to see the stars.

"*Perhaps we are here in order to say: house / bridge, fountain, gate, pitch-*
er, fruit-tree, window— / …but to say them, you must understand, / oh
to say them more intensely than the Things themselves / ever dreamed of
existing."
   This is Rilke talking.
   If I dared to revise Rilke, I would cut the word "Perhaps."
   No, Rilke, "we are here."
   I carry Rilke's words with me every time I go into the classroom,
every time I go into and go beneath the page.

The page is like a sheet of ice on the river.

Once you fall in, once you go under, there's no turning back.

Or else.

Remember Orpheus.

But even in the end, even after his head had been severed from his body and was floating down the river, bobbing up and down on top of the waves, the head of Orpheus—it kept on singing.

I want the students to feel that they can come to the page unafraid, to feel they can say anything.

The freedom there in that.

That there is no right or wrong in a poem.

Poetry, I want them to know, is not a spelling test.

Write.

Right on.

That is the right answer, the rightest response.

I also want the students to come to the page like God did when God separated the darkness from the light.

To write as if the hand you're writing with is the hand of God.

"I want a watch made from the bones in God's hands."

John Rybicki.

"Or the bet is off."

I've Got the Whole World
in My Hands

I HOLD UP MY hands, palms facing out, so that everyone can see.

"Look at my hands," I tell them. "Tell me what you see."

"I see your hands," one boy says.

"Good," I say. I nod my head. Then I ask, "What else?"

One girl tells me, "You've got blue ink all over your hands, Mr. Pete."

She tries not to laugh. She laughs. The whole class laughs.

I turn my hands back toward me so I can see what she is seeing, so I can see what the whole class is laughing about.

I hadn't noticed, maybe because I'm so used to it, but it's true. I do have a blob of blue ink smeared all over my hand.

"It's from writing," I tell them.

Then I say, "What else do you see?"

"You've got a ring on your one hand," one girl points out.

"I do," I say, as if I am getting married. "Actually," I tell her, "I've got two rings on my finger."

I slip and twist the rings until they climb up around the mountain of my knuckle and then I hold them up for them to see.

"One is my wedding ring," I tell them, "and the other one is my grandmother's wedding ring."

"Why do you have your grandma's wedding ring?" one girl asks.

"Because she gave it to me when she was still alive," I say.

The sadness of this sentence begins to get to me, so I quickly move on and I keep keeping on.

It's like Mark Strand wrote in his poem "Keeping Things Whole."

> *We all have reasons*
> *for moving.*
> *I move*
> *to keep things whole.*

I move on.

I move my hands down lower, down close to one boy's face.

"Look closely at my hands," I tell him. "Tell me what you see."

"I see lines," this boy says.

I cup my hands, curl up my fingertips a bit so that the lines this boy sees curl up into wrinkles.

"Now what do you see?" I say.

"I see wrinkles."

I shake my head.

"Rivers," I tell him.

"Rivers?"

"Yes, the wrinkles are actually rivers."

"Where?" he says. "How?" he wonders.

"They're right here," I tell him, "in the palms of my hands."

I see fish, I tell them this.

"I see fish swimming in the rivers in the palms of my hands."

Goldfish.

Boldfish.

Stonefish.

Fish with wings.

Fish that talk.

Fish that walk on top of the water.

"I see fish," I say, "that can sing!"

"You're just messing with us, Mr. Pete," one boy says. "You're just making that all up."

I look this boy square in the eye. I place my right hand across my heart.

"I'm just telling you," I tell him, "what I see. It's up to you whether or not you believe it."

Hold out your hands, I tell them.

"Tell me what you see in the palms of your hands."

I tell them to look with their magic pencils. I remind them that their magic pencils aren't just pencils.

"Your magic pencil is a magnifying glass," I say. "It makes small things look big. It helps you to see things that you might not otherwise see."

Picture a room full of second graders gazing down into the palms of their hands.

I've got them.

I've got them right where I want them.

Eating right from the palms of my hands.

Like birds.

Like birds that, once they are fed, they will sing.

Hear them sing.

Roar.

Soar.

In the palm of my hand I see stars that are singing in the sky.

In the palm of my hand I see a flower that is glowing.

In the palm of my hand I see a volcano erupting.

In the palm of my hand I see Easter eggs and a moon shining.

In the palm of my hand I see rocks and fire and there is water rotating in my hand because of a tornado in my hand. I have power in the palm of my hand just like in any other palm.

One boy sees rocket blasts, butterflies, sharks, boats, money, basketballs, frogs, power, numbers, hawks, books, the state of Indiana, dots, moons, yards, jump ropes, stars, clovers, trees, and a box filled with mud.

In the palm of my hand a spider is crawling and it bit me. Ouch, that hurt! Ouch, that hurt!

In the palm of my hand I have magical powers, I have God's power, I am a tornado, I have a cyclone in the palm of my hand.

In the palm of my hand I see a whole village of people and fish and moon and stars.

In the palm of my hand I am baking a cake and reading a book and writing a story. Plus my hand is so fun it plays when I play. I can talk to my hand.

In the palm of my hand I see a hundred-dollar bill.

I see a seahorse and a pink flower and a dancing dog in the palm of my hand.

In the palm of my hand I can see a planet with an asteroid on it and a person is on it too. He slid down the asteroid and then it rolled off the planet and went into another one. Then he goes back to his spaceship.

In the palm of my hand I see people riding on bikes. It is spring and they are wearing shorts and two boys are fighting. Their names are Tom and Jerry. They were fighting over a bike.

I see a fish on the moon that is as big as a tree. The eye in the palm of my hand, it looks like a star.

In the palm of my hand I see an angel flying with a fairy that has sparkling light hair and a pink dress who is dancing with her husband and is having the greatest time of her life.

When I look into the palm of my hand I see two trees and I can see four rings and a jump rope that ten girls are playing with and I see a basketball hoop that six boys are playing with and I can feel glad when I touch my hand.

My hand has stripes that is a tiger shivering.

I see a poem in the palm of my hand.

I think I'll end this section with that (I'll let this line be the last thought: a poem in the palm of the hand).

It puts me, all of it, in the mind of the Wallace Stevens poem "Of Mere Being":

> *The palm at the end of the mind,*
> *Beyond the last thought, rises*
> *In the bronze decor,*
>
> *A gold-feathered bird*
> *Sings in the palm, without human meaning,*
> *Without human feeling, a foreign song.*
>
> *You know then that it is not the reason*
> *That makes us happy or unhappy.*
> *The bird sings. Its feathers shine.*
>
> *The palm stands on the edge of space.*
> *The wind moves slowly in the branches.*
> *The bird's fire-fangled feathers dangle down.*

Like Stevens writes, "*The bird sings. Its feathers shine.*"

"*The wind moves slowly through the branches.*"

Like the wind, there is an invisible force that ruffles the pages of the papers that I gather up at the end of each class.

A lingering, a resonance, "*Beyond the last thought...*"

Something heard.

A church bell ringing.

"*...a foreign song.*"

When I read this poem out loud to the kids, when I ask them, "What's this poem about? What's this poem saying?" this is what they say.

They say, "It's about our magic pencils."

They say, "It's about using your imagination."

They say, "It's about what you are teaching us, Mr. Pete."

They say, "It's about being transformed."

There's that word again!

They say, "It's about singing."

There's that word too!

They say, "It's about you, Mr. Pete."

Mr. Pete?

I say, "What do you mean, it's about Mr. Pete?"

They say, "You're the one who wrote it, Mr. Pete. Why don't you tell us what the poem is about?"

I say, "What makes you think I wrote this poem?"

They say, "You mean you didn't write that poem?"

And what I say to this is, "I wish."

I wish my hands could touch the moon and erase the clouds on gray skies and I wish my hands could catch a falling star and make a wish that all these things would come true. And I wish my hands could shake hands with my grandfather and I wish I could wipe the tears from my grandmother's face and I wish my hands could make music when I play my air guitar. I wish my hands could heal the sick and when I rub my hands together I wish a white bird would appear and fly up to God and tell Him that I think of Him often and I wish that when I snap my fingers I could resurrect the dead. I wish my hands could dunk a basketball and I wish my hands could throw a baseball one hundred miles an hour. I wish my hands could straighten the trees that have fallen in the storm. And I wish my hands could stop the bombs that are blowing up this world.

These are just a few of the things that I tell the students I wish that my hands could do.

We talk too about what our hands can do, what they do do, what is possible in this world.

We make a list, we build a wall of words—"What kind of words?" I ask them. Verbs is what they say—about all those things, all those actions, that our hands can do:

Hit. Slap. Dribble. Touch. Feel. Point. Lift. Play. Draw. Make. Write.

Yes, hands can make things right, I think this to myself.

What else?

Hands that hold. That shove. That punch. That pull. That fix. That help. Hands that take.

Hands that give. Hands that reach.

Drum. Beat. Pound.

Hands that clap. Hands that pet. Hands that feed.

Hands that transform (there's that word again!).

Hands that shake. Hands that carry. Hands that throw. Shoot. Hands that steer. Hands that steal.

"There is no end to what hands can do," I say.

I look at my hands.

My hands are doing a dance in front of me as I speak.

My hands are hands that talk.

I close my fingers in to meet up with my thumb.

"What is my hand now?" I ask them.

I move my hand back and forth, open and then shut.

"It looks like a puppet," they say.

I make a sound with my mouth. I move my hands to that sound.

"Look," I tell them. "My hands can even talk."

Now that we see and have heard about the seemingly infinite possibilities that we hold in the palms of our hands, I tell them to pick up a pencil.

We add that verb to our list: pick.

To pick up.

To pick a number.

One boy says, "To pick your nose."

How can I not laugh?

I laugh.

"To pick your butt," says another.

"Your pencils," I say. "Pick up your pencils.

I tell them, "Put your pencils to the paper."

I say, "I see a poem in the palms of your hands."

A poem waiting to be made.

Here is some of what they make:

> *My hands play baseball*
> *with my brothers and with my cousins*
> *at my new house. My hands*

pick up a cheeseburger
so I can eat it. My hands
play my GameCube
for six hours straight
until my hands turn purple.
My hands can pick up
a microphone and sing in it
until I run out of breath.

My hands can write,
can pick up an ice cream cone,
play basketball, video games,
eat dinner. They can put
on a hat, my backpack, color,
play cards, get me dressed. I can
write with my hands,
read a book, cook, put a tape in
the VCR, cut on the radio,
cut on the TV, play on
the playground, talk on the phone.
My hands are my friends.

My hands punch on the punching bag.
My hands help me to write.
My hands help me to ride a bike.
My hands help me to pick up a pickle.
My hands help me wipe away my tears.
My hands help me scrub the dirt off my face.

My hands have been with me
when I was not even born. I get to
pick up things.
I get to put down things. My
hands are like rivers,
they flow with blood
like a stream. Some people don't
have hands.
I am happy that I do.

My hands
help me
read books.
My hands
help me
to feel.

My hands made a card for my daddy when it was his birth-
day. My hand wrote a poem for my grandma.
My hands touched the water when it was warm.
My hands picked up the bunny when it was scared.

I am proud of what my hands can do. My hands can move,
write, throw.
My hands can do anything I tell them to.
But I am scared. What if I lose them?
What am I going to do?

What Have I Just Done?

I PICK UP WITH my hand a black magic marker, then I make with my hand a downward slanted line across the classroom's white magic marker board.

"What," I ask the students, "have I just done?"

It's a simple question, yes?

But it's a simple question that is fishing for some not-so-simple answers.

"You've made a black line on the board," one boy tells me, simply so.

"That's true," I say. "I *have* made a black line on the white marker board. But what else?"

I tell them to look at what I've just done with their third eye.

I tell them to see the possibilities.

"What," I say, "might this black line be the beginning of?"

"It could be the side of a mountain," someone says.

"Good," I say to this. "What else?"

"It could be the roof of a house."

"Excellent, excellent."

I say it twice. Nod my head.

"Keep it going," I tell them.

One boy says, "It looks like a lightning bolt without the zigzags."

Someone else says, "It could be a tree falling over in a storm."

"You're on roll now, boys and girls," I tell them. "Don't stop now. Keep the ball rolling."

One girl says, "It looks like the number one falling backwards."

One boy says, "It looks like a snake."

Someone else says, "It could be a star shooting across the night sky."

Someone else adds, "It could be a cane that some old man uses to help himself walk."

This goes on for some time.

This line on the board, it goes on forever.

"Could be a fishing pole," one boy says.

"Or," says another, "it could be the barrel of a gun."

"It could be," one girl says, and scratches at her head, "the shadow of a pencil."

"That's beautiful," I say. "What's the pencil doing?" I ask.

"It's just laying there 'cause it lost its magic," she explains.

"You know how and why a magic pencil loses its magic?" I say.

She shakes her head no.

"A magic pencil loses its magic power," I warn them, "when that magic pencil doesn't get used enough by its owner."

I tell them, "The more you use your magic pencil, the more magical that magic pencil will become."

"I know what it is," one girl says, raising her hand wildly in the air to get my attention. "I think it looks like a magic pencil waiting for someone to pick it up."

"On that note," I tell them, "I think it's time to pick up our pencils."

"It's time," I say, "to turn that piece of paper sitting on your desk into more than just a piece of paper sitting on your desk."

"To transform it," one girl says, saying what I'm thinking.

"Yes, exactly," I say.

There's that word again!

"We start with nothing," I say, "and end up with something that didn't even know that it existed. That," I say, "is the beauty of a pencil."

"We start with just mud," I say, "and we end up standing inside a mud house."

Our words become the house we live in.

There's Hafiz again.

To make it a house—a house made out of mud, made out of words or wood, hay or brick: to make a house that will not blow down.

A thing of steel that will not bend or break.

Or if it broke, it would "break into blossom."

Like a flower that does not wilt.

Good poets imitate.

Great poets steal.

I've already said this.

It was T.S. Eliot who said this first.

I stole the idea of drawing a line on the blackboard from a poem by ex-Detroiter Philip Levine.

The poem is called "M. Degas Teaches Art & Science at Durfee Intermediate School—Detroit, 1942."

Here it is in its entirety:

> *He made a line on the blackboard,*
> *one bold stroke from right to left*
> *diagonally downward and stood back*
> *to ask, looking as always at no one*
> *in particular, "What have I done?"*

From the back of the room Freddie
shouted, "You've broken a piece
of chalk." M. Degas did not smile.
"What have I done?" he repeated.
The most intellectual students
looked down to study their desks
except for Gertrude Bimmler, who raised
her hand before she spoke. "M. Degas,
you have created the hypotenuse
of an isosceles triangle." Degas mused.
Everyone knew that Gertrude could not
be incorrect. "It is possible,"
Louis Warshowsky added precisely,
"that you have begun to represent
the roof of a barn." I remember
that it was exactly twenty minutes
past eleven, and I thought at worst
this would go on another forty
minutes. It was early April,
the snow had all but melted on
the playgrounds, the elms and maples
bordering the cracked walks shivered
in the new winds, and I believed
that before I knew it I'd be
swaggering to the candy store
for a Milky Way. M. Degas
pursed his lips, and the room
stilled until the long hand
of the clock moved to twenty-one

as though in complicity with Gertrude,
who added confidently, "You've begun
to separate the dark from the dark."
I looked back for help, but now
the trees bucked and quaked, and I
knew this could go on forever.

Who, I cannot help but wonder, is the Gertrude Bimmler of the group? And who is more like the speaker in this poem, the daydreamer who is dreaming of being anywhere but here inside this classroom, being asked, on this budding spring day, to answer the seemingly simple question posed by M. Degas:

"What have I done?"

I can only hope that, one day, a poem might be written by one of these students with the words "Mr. Pete Teaches Us…" in its title.

It is my hope to get these young poets to think beyond and above the straight and narrow line.

It is my hope to fill their ever-expandable minds with nothing but possibility.

To get them to see the infinite in the inanimate thing.

To find the pleasure in the pencil.

To speak the dream before the reason.

To believe in what can and what cannot be seen.

In short—I don't think that I'm asking too much here. I hate to seem greedy. I already want so much—:

I want to leave a mark.

I know for sure what I don't want to do.

I don't want to be like the teacher, the exasperated old nun, in this poem by Paul Zimmer:

At the blackboard I had missed
Five number problems in a row,
And was about to foul a sixth,
When the old, exasperated nun
Began to pound my head against
My six mistakes. When I cried,
She threw me back into my seat,
Where I hid my head and swore
That very day I'd be a poet,
And curse her yellow teeth with this.

Both of these poems are what I like to call "On Becoming a Poet" poems.

Levine's M. Degas and Zimmer's "exasperated nun" sit on opposite ends of the table, but they are both sources of inspiration to the poet-to-be (i.e. the poet that doesn't yet know he is a poet).

In both poems, the poet/speaker is trapped: a caged brain.

M. Degas uses the mystery of the everyday, of the mundane—a diagonal line chalked on a blackboard—to get his students to see that even the most seemingly meaningless gesture can become charged with meaning. In this poem, the blackboard is a night sky with stars too plentiful to count.

In the Zimmer poem, the blackboard is a blank wall.

But that wall, in the end, the speaker in this poem—the pencil in his hand, it is a hammer, it is a maestro's baton—he breaks it down with his song.

Finding Your Voice

I WALK INTO GOLIGHTLY one Tuesday morning to see and to hear that Mrs. Sturgill, one of the teachers, has lost her voice. How, you might be wondering, can a teacher possibly teach (second graders, no less!) if she cannot speak?

It's a good question.

But what you need to know about Mrs. Sturgill is this. Her classroom is more of a chapel than it is a classroom. It's a chapel, quiet, calm, when quiet and calm is what is needed. But it is, at other times during the day, a chapel with pogo sticks and a trampoline sitting smack dab in the middle of the room (when the classroom needs to be transformed—there's that word again!—into a playroom, or a funhouse, the kind of place where a pencil is more than just a pencil: where a pencil is a toy).

When I ask Mrs. Sturgill this same question, she goes silently over to the magic marker board and writes, she tells me that, "I am writing what I have to say down."

In other words, she is using the written word to speak.

The magic marker in Mrs. Sturgill's hand isn't just an ordinary magic marker.

This magic marker is Mrs. Sturgill's voice.

Mrs. Sturgill's voice isn't lost, it's still there, though now she has to use her hands in order to speak.

Her hands write down the words that her mouth cannot say.

Her hands also are pointing to point to the students who have their hands in the air.

"Who stole Mrs. Sturgill's voice?" I ask them. "Did a burglar crawl in through her window at night and steal it from her mouth?"

"No!"

"Did the moon reach through Mrs. Sturgill's bedroom window because it was jealous of how beautiful her voice is and say to Mrs. Sturgill, 'Give me that! I'll teach you not to sing in the morning when the sun comes up!' Is that what happened to Mrs. Sturgill's voice?"

"No!"

"Do you think that maybe Mrs. Sturgill, without even knowing it, in the middle of the night, hiccupped and then by accident she maybe swallowed her voice down into her belly, where it's sitting there trapped like Pinocchio in the belly of the whale?"

"No!"

"Then what?" I ask them. "How does someone *lose* their voice?"

One boy says, "It's something called laryngitis." He points to the magic marker board where the word LARYNGITIS is written, in Mrs. Sturgill's handwriting, in big letters across the top.

It is the word of the day.

"But that still doesn't tell me *how* somebody loses their voice," I tell them. "Where," I say, "does the voice go? Is there some lost voice lost-and-found somewhere we can go to look for it?"

"No!"

"Did her voice just decide that it was going to run away from home, so it packed its bags and snuck out the window and then hopped a train heading down to Texas? Is that what happened?"

"No!"

"Or maybe it was a cat that climbed into Mrs. Sturgill's bed last night and mistook her voice for a can of tuna fish and ate it all up. You think that's what happened to Mrs. Sturgill's voice?"

"No!"

"Then what? Who can tell me what happened to Mrs. Sturgill's voice? How are we going to help Mrs. Sturgill get it back?"

Nobody says anything. It's as though every one of us in the room, at this moment, has lost our voice.

So I decide to tell them a story—what better way to break the silence—about a bluebird that woke up one fine morning, just like Mrs. Sturgill did this morning, to find that he had lost his voice.

It goes like this:

Bluebird was singing in a tree.

Singing was what Bluebird liked to do best.

He was a good singer.

His song was a beautiful song.

Nobody had ever taught Bluebird how to sing. He just opened up his mouth and the song of Bluebird singing came singing out.

Bluebird sang when the sun rose up in the morning; it was so beautiful the way the light wiped away the darkness. And then Bluebird kept singing till the sun set in the night.

At night was when Bluebird went to sleep.

At night Bluebird did not sing.

Nighttime was the time when Bluebird and his beautiful singing rested in silence.

Bluebird's eyes had never looked too long at the moon and the stars shining down from the night sky above.

The moon and the stars never got to hear Bluebird's beautiful song.

The sun would sometimes whisper up to the moon and stars, "You don't know what you're missing. Bluebird's song is the most beautiful sound of all. It is even more beautiful than the sound that a river makes when it is running out to sea."

The moon and the stars loved the sound that rivers made when they were running out to sea.

They loved the sound that children liked to make, the oohs and the aahs, when the moon was big and full and shining, or when a star shot burning hot across the sky.

The moon and the stars had heard about Bluebird's beautiful song because the sun was always bragging.

When Bluebird sang, everyone who heard it could not help but stop doing whatever they were doing.

Cooks stopped cooking.

Teachers stopped teaching.

Barbers stopped barbering.

Barking dogs stopped barking.

Even the sun sometimes stayed in its place in the sky.

When you heard Bluebird singing, you could not help but lift your eyes up toward the sky, up toward the heavens, to see who was the singer of such a beautiful song.

When Bluebird sang, whoever heard his song, you could not hear it and be unhappy.

Unhappiness was not possible when Bluebird's song was being sung.

But one morning, when Bluebird woke up with the rising light of the sun, when Bluebird opened up his beak to sing, "Good day, good morning, it's good to be alive," no sound came singing out.

"My song!" Bluebird cried out, though nobody heard him say it. "Where has it gone?"

Bluebird tried again to sing: he opened up his mouth wide, as wide as it would open, but still no sound, no song, came singing out.

"My voice!" Bluebird once again cried out, and once again nobody heard him say it. "I've lost my voice! Somebody has stolen my voice!"

Bluebird stood up in his nest and looked down in his nest as if his song was a thing that he was hoping to be able to see it sitting there, like an egg that hadn't yet hatched.

There was no such thing, no song, or egg, sitting in the bottom of his nest.

And so Bluebird flew up to the top of the tree to see what he might be able to see from up there.

He could see the tops of other trees. He could see the sun rising up over the river. He could see the river flowing blue below. He could see other birds and he could hear their other bird songs. But he could not see, and nobody could hear, his beautiful bluebird song.

"My song!" he cried out again, in silence. "My beautiful song!"

Even the sun that morning seemed not to shine as bright and yellow.

The world was not the same beautiful world without Bluebird's beautiful song heard in it.

Bluebird did what he could without his voice, without his bluebird song.

He flew around looking for something or somebody who might know something about what had happened to his lost song.

He asked around to other birds, but the other birds just kept on singing.

He saw his friend Squirrel, who was busy collecting acorns in the park, and Bluebird flew down to see if Squirrel had anything to say.

Bluebird could not talk. He had no voice to talk with. He had no song.

So Bluebird jumped up and down, he shook his head, he beat his bluebird wings against the ground, until finally Squirrel said to Bluebird, "Bluebird, what is the matter with your voice?"

This was not the answer that Bluebird was looking for—though it was the answer that he heard, time and time again, all day long, from his friends Fox and Butterfly and Chipmunk and Dog and Cat and Muskrat and Snake.

They all asked the same question when they saw Bluebird jumping up and down and shaking his head and beating his blue wings against the ground.

"Bluebird," they said, "what is the matter with your voice?"

None of them had the answer that Bluebird went out looking for. Bluebird himself did not know the answer.

Bluebird did not know what to do.

So Bluebird did what he could do: he flew back up to his nest in the tree and he looked at the world around him. Even without his song, the world was still a beautiful place. It was filled with beautiful things: the leaves of the trees, the lights of the city, the blue sky about to turn dark, the sun that was just now about to set.

"Goodbye, Sun," Bluebird said without actually saying it. He sang without actually singing.

He heard other sounds that he thought were beautiful sounds: like the sound the river made as it ran out to sea. Or the sound that the wind made when it blew through the trees. Like the sound and the songs of other birds singing.

And later on, when the sun finally sank down completely behind the tops of the trees, Bluebird lifted up his gaze and watched as the moon and the night sky and the billions of stars took over what the sun and the daylight had left them.

"Oh, what a gift," was what Bluebird thought, and he wished he could sing to say it.

The moon, in Bluebird's eyes, it looked to him like a wide open mouth that was made to sing.

Bluebird lifted his beak up toward the moon and he opened it so that if he had a voice to sing with he would've sang long and loud about the beauty of the moon.

The beauty of the stars.

Each star deserved its own song.

But still, no sound came singing out from Bluebird's mouth.

Now, in this silence, it was Bluebird's heart that was doing the singing.

Bluebird could hear it, that sound inside of his bluebird body, and it was a sound that he knew was beautiful.

"Maybe the moon can hear what nobody else can hear," was what Bluebird thought.

"Maybe the stars can hear," was what Bluebird hoped, "what right now only I can hear me singing."

Oh, the thought of this, the possibility of this—this made Bluebird as happy as a bird can be.

He was right now the happiest bird alive, even if he couldn't sing and bring his song of happiness out into the world.

Bluebird sang in the silence.

Bluebird drank in the silence.

And the moon, which was perfectly full, it shined down a spotlight of light upon Bluebird singing this new song.

And when this light shined into Bluebird's wide open mouth, the sound of his singing, the sound of his voice, his song, it came once again singing out, so that the moon and every star in the sky, every stone at the bottom of the river, could hear this song.

Bluebird sang and he sang and he kept on singing all through the night and into the next morning. He could not stop. He would not stop. He sang until the moon and the stars came back into the sky. He sang a different song for each of the stars.

Listen.

Do you hear that sound?

Listen again.

Is that the sound of Bluebird singing?

Is that the beating of your own heart?

To seek and to find and to see what is beautiful in your own life, through your own eyes, the beauty of the everyday.

The sun and the moon and the stars are the same no matter where you stand gazing up.

It's not where you live.

It's how you live.

My wife once said this to me.

To find yourself in the arms of your beloved.

To be loved.

To be loving.

That's where the voice is when we think that it's lost.

That is the source of our song.

Mr. Pete and the Twelve-Legged Purple Octopus: Revisited

So I GO INTO Golightly on Tuesday, May tenth, ten minutes late.

"Sorry I'm so late, boys and girls," I say, huffing and puffing to catch my breath. "But really, it wasn't my fault."

"What happened, Mr. Pete?"

"You don't want to know," I tell them. I shake my head. "You wouldn't believe me if I told you."

"Tell us, Mr. Pete! Tell us!"

"I don't know if I should..."

"Please, Mr. Pete!"

"Are you *sure* you want to know?" I say.

"We do! We do!"

So I do.

I tell them.

I tell them, "It's a beautiful day."

This, they already know.

"Look outside," I say. I point with my hand out the window at the beautiful blue skies. I tell them, "A man born blind, without eyes, would be able to see the beauty of this beautiful day."

This is how I begin my story of why I, Mr. Pete, was late, once again, for school.

What I do not tell them is that, as a boy, when I used to walk to school, I always used to get to school late, even though I always left the house with plenty of time to get to school before the tardy bell rang, because I was always getting sidetracked, I was always getting distracted, by things that I'd see or even sometimes just hear on my way to school.

A leaf falling to the ground, for instance.

Or a dog barking.

Or a bird singing somewhere out of sight.

Any of these things (and others too: a worm trying to worm its way across the sidewalk; an oddly shaped constellation of clouds; an airplane's exhaust chalking the sky) would stop me in my tracks.

And then, before I knew it, I would hear, off in the distance, the sound of the school bell ringing, which would break me out of my reverie, and then I would run, huffing and puffing, off to school.

Late.

Tardy.

Delinquent.

When I'd walk into the classroom, all of the other kids would already have their pencils in their hands, working on their morning bell work.

In fact, I was late so often that, when I did get to school on time, I would often forget the words to the Pledge of Allegiance.

It was my third grade teacher, Mrs. Fortner, who warned my mother that she "had a poet on her hands."

My mother took this warning not as a curse, but as a blessing. Bless me for having such a mother.

Anyhow, back to the story of why I was ten minutes late, again, to teach my classes at Golightly.

I was, I tell the students, a few minutes early, and I was sitting in my car, outside of school, right out there on Ferry Street, killing time, listening to some tunes on the radio, clearing my head, getting ready to come in to teach a lesson on the beauty and efficiency of haiku—"Who," I might have asked, "has heard of the word *haiku* before?"—when I heard something very, very strange.

Something very, very scary.

It sounded like someone was banging their fist on the top of my car.

It sounded like some*thing* was banging some*thing* on the top of my car.

A hammer, I say.

Or a bucket filled with steel.

"Do you know what it was?" I ask the students.

"What? What was it?"

"You don't want to know," I say.

"Tell us!" they say. "Tell us!"

So I keep on with my telling.

I tell them that I was scared, that when I heard what I heard, I also heard my heart thumping in fear on the inside of my chest.

"I thought the sky was falling," I say. "You know, like that story about the chicken who runs around town telling everyone that the sky is falling, the sky is falling, even though it isn't? I thought for a second that maybe the chicken was right, or that the chicken running around town like he was a chicken with his head cut off was like a prophet chicken who had the ability to see into the future."

It's true: it sounded like the sky was falling.

"But the sky," I tell them. "It was not falling."

But there *was* something on the top of my car.

I was too scared to look.

I didn't want to see what it was even though I wanted to know what it was.

When whatever it was did decide to show its face, I did not want to look.

But I did.

I looked.

This is what I saw.

I saw a face.

It was the kind of face only a mother could love.

It was big.

It was purple.

I ask them, "Can you guess whose face this was?"

As if I am asking them to tell me what is the color of the sky, they all cry out, "The twelve-legged octopus!"

And, of course, they're right.

"He came back!" one boy says as if he is talking about an old friend who left without saying goodbye.

"Yes, he most certainly did," I say.

One girl says, "What did he say?"

One boy asks, "What did he want?"

"Why, Mr. Pete," they all want to know, "was he banging on the top of your car?"

These are just some of the things that the kids wanted to know about the return of the twelve-legged purple octopus.

So I tell them what I know.

I tell them, "He didn't want to go dancing."

I tell them, "He didn't sing me a song."

I tell them, "He didn't want to go fishing, either."

"What did he want, then?" someone asks.

"I'll tell you," I tell them. "But like I told him," I say, "you're not gonna believe it when I say it."

"Say it!" they say.

"Tell us!"

So I do.

Two words.

Three syllables.

A poem.

"A poem?" they say.

"A poem," I say back.

I explain that, "That twelve-legged purple octopus with the goldfish-orange top hat who was doing all sorts of tricks—back flips and front flips and sideways flips and pogo-stick-flips—on that one-wheeled unicycle of a bike of his. You remember him?" I say. "That twelve-legged octopus with the three teeth and the stanky breath and the kiss that was wet and slobbery like a grandma's kiss? Remember?"

They do.

They remember him down to the littlest detail.

"He wanted to show me," I tell them, "a poem."

"He wanted to give to me," I say, "a poem."

"A poem," I say, "for me to read to you."

I reach my hand into my back trouser pocket.

I fish out a piece of paper, folded and wet.

I unfold it.

I hold it up for all eyes to see.

And then I read.

I read what it says.

I read what only a twelve-legged purple octopus could say.

I am a twelve-legged purple octopus. I am riding down the street on a unicycle. I can do tricks on my one-wheeled bike. I am as big as a second-grade classroom. I can't see so good but boy can I hear. I can hear Mr. Pete when he is sitting quiet in his car. I can hear the ocean calling me to come back home. Goodbye. Good day. See you next time. Until then, be good. That's the end of my story.

"And then what happened, Mr. Pete?"

"Did he kiss you goodbye?" one girl asks.

One boy asks, "Did his breath still stink real bad?"

I tell them the truth.

No, he didn't kiss me.

I didn't get a chance to smell his breath.

And then he was gone.

Yes, that twelve-legged purple octopus with the goldfish-orange top hat with the green fuzzy feather dangling down off the top of that hat, he read his poem to me and then he left.

He got back up on that one-wheeled unicycle of a bike of his.

"But this time," I tell them, "he didn't ride away."

What did he do?

No, a limousine did not come to pick this twelve-legged purple octopus up.

He did not slide sideways into my car and drive away (for one thing, he never would have fit). And I don't think that an octopus, even one with twelve legs, would know how to drive a stick shift.

But what he did do was bounce.

He bounced back up onto the top of my car.

He bounced up and down on top of my car on that one-wheeled, unicycle bike.

He bounced, and he bounced again, as if my car was a trampoline, and then he bounced all the way up into the blue of the sky.

The blue of the sky, when that twelve-legged purple octopus bounced up into it, I am telling you right now: it splashed.

It splashed like a river or a lake or an ocean or a sea would splash when you throw a stone in it.

What I am telling you now is that the blue of the sky, it turned into the blue of the ocean: the sky was *transformed* (there's that word yet again!) into the blue of the sea.

And that twelve-legged purple octopus with the goldfish-orange top hat and the stanky breath and the kiss that was as wet and slobbery as a grandma's, just like that, he swam away. He went back home.

And that is the end of this story.

Poetry Is Good Food

Ink runs from the corners of my mouth.
There is no happiness like mine.
I have been eating poetry.
  Mark Strand, "Eating Poetry"

I KNOW ABOUT THAT happiness. There are days when the ink runs from the corners of my mouth and I can cry out, as Strand does at the end of his poem, "I am a new man."

But there are days when I'd rather watch others eat, when I like to stand back and watch that ink run down from the lips of the Detroit Public Schools children that I teach through my work as a poet-in-the-schools with the InsideOut Literary Arts Project.

I have taught "Eating Poetry" to such ink-lipped children—children who have been dogged and belittled for not measuring up, for underachieving, for failing in the mechanical eyes of standardized measures of intelligence.

I am here to tell you that none of the children I teach are failures. It's true that many of them live beneath the poverty level, that most of them are eligible to receive free breakfast and lunch, that many of them come from broken homes and drag in the stresses that come from growing up poor and sometimes hungry.

There are places for kids to go, for their parents to take them to, if they are hungry: food banks, community centers, etc. But the hunger I want to talk about now is a hunger, an undernourishment, that leaves not just the belly empty, but the soul, the spirit.

I often tell my students, "Poetry is good food." I am leaning, of course, on the Campbell's Soup claim that soup is good food, which it is. But the language of poetry is its own kind of sweet, medicinal broth.

For eight years, I worked as the writer-in-residence at the Golightly Educational Center in Detroit. Here I had the pleasure and privilege to work with hundreds of students year after year, some since they were second graders still struggling to hold a pencil up until they were seventh graders, whose bigger problems involved issues such as drugs and broken preteen hearts. But after a few years of weekly doses of reading and writing and eating poetry, my job was easy. As easy as it is to bring a silver spoon up to your own mouth, I'd walk into the school with new twists on old recipes for soup: Merwin's Meatball Minestrone, Bishop's Black Bean, Levine and Lorca's Duende Lentil Combo. I am a proud cook in the poetry soup kitchen when I tell you that the kids ate it up. And the memory of the meals lasts in the way that sensory experiences always do: they last through the promise of their own renewal.

Poetry lives, I believe, in the heart of every child. But this sentence falls short of saying what I'm trying to say and is said best through the poem of the child.

Hear the child.

Poetry Lives
by Troinana Barnett

Poetry lives
in the strings
of a guitar,
the peak
of a mountain.

Poetry lives
in the sass
of a girl's walk,
the wishes
of a dying child.

Poetry lives
in the stretch
of an eyelash,
the flash of
a blinding light.

Poetry lives
in every rhyme
every melody
we speak,
every line
every stanza
we write.

Poetry lives and poetry lives on and lasts because poetry offers students a non-linear path into its woods. Its difference—the way it looks on the page, the sounds of words carefully chosen, the musicality of its broken lines—is what draws a child inside. Children, by nature, are naturally curious creatures. We learn the world by doing our best to grab at it and put it into our mouth. The same can be said for how children take an almost organic liking to poetry, as long as it is offered up without restriction, without a belief that poems only mean one thing.

When confronted with the question, "What is a poem?" young marvel Eddie Stewart understands the multitudes that a poem can contain.

What Is a Poem?
by Eddie Stewart

A poem is a ball of fire
lifting into the sky.

No. A poem is a girl with hair
long enough to climb.

A poem is a car speeding down the road
going past the speed limit.

A poem is a flower blooming
faster than all the other flowers.

No. A poem is a lesson that you will
always remember.

A poem is a mother bird
teaching her babies how to fly.

A poem is the happiest mother in the world
on Mother's Day.

No. A poem is a man riding a dragon saying
"This is the best day of my life."

Hey, don't you know that you can rise up
to become whatever you want.

Did you know the world is a better
place with you on it.

I'm Eddie Stewart and I want everyone
to get off their feet and be as happy as you can be.

Everyone, I want you to share some
happy times in your life with friends.

Don't be afraid, you can make a bigger difference.
Remember: you are a Queen bee watching over the hive.

I like to make sure that the poems are tangible objects, so I begin by passing out copies of the day's poem to each student so that they can hold the poem's words in their hands. Then I like to read the poem out loud so that the poem's cadence can cleanly enter their ears. Then it's time to put the poem into their mouths, so I invite students to take turns reading a line, a stanza, sometimes an entire poem, so that their tongue can taste it. We do this for as long as there are mouths wanting to open, to speak the poem into being.

I like Gertrude Stein's claim that "children themselves are poetry." Poems, like children, live. Poets, like parents, live through their poems. When I asked students recently what they like most about poetry, what many of them said was: "In a poem, there is no right or wrong. The poem is what it is."

To see the child the way the child sees poetry: the way a child is what a child is.

Like a poem is.

Where much is possible and there is much for us to see.

Like the blue of the sky.

Or a window.

An open door for us to walk through.

A house for us all to live in.